Contents

Part 1 Real Estate: The Asset Class

Part 2 Managing Performance

COMMERCIAL REAL ESTATE INVESTMENT

by

ANDREW BAUM

A division of Reed Business Information
ESTATES GAZETTE
151 WARDOUR STREET, LONDON W1F 8BN

First published in 2000 by Chandos Publishing (Oxford) Limited
This reformatted edition published by Estates Gazette in September 2002

ISBN 0 7282 0389 8

Reprinted 2007, 2008

Printed in Great Britain by Bell & Bain Ltd., Glasgow

Foreword

For investors, property has been something of a puzzle. Against its large share of national wealth, the representation of property in multi-asset portfolios is not only low, but has fallen to one-third of what it was twenty years ago. On the available evidence (its accuracy in turn a subject of debate) property's risk and return history refuses to fit neatly into the framework of modern portfolio theory through which investors view the world. Still worse, through much of the last twenty years property has failed to meet, either in absolute terms or relative to alternative investments, the simple return thresholds investors need to beat. And, in an era obsessed with the globalisation and transparency of investment, property markets are still heavily divided by national differences in statute, regulation and culture; accurate international comparisons are at best expensive, at worst impossible to come by. Property has, indeed, looked in danger of becoming an afterthought in the asset allocations of major investors.

There is, fortunately, a brighter, more interesting side to the picture. A run of satisfactory rates of return through the last five years – in the UK and many other countries – has revived flagging investor interest. And, thanks to a burgeoning, perhaps even blossoming, in commercial property research since the mid-1980s, property investment is far better understood and far better managed than it was twenty years ago. Many of the problems which were associated with property investment at that time have found workable (if rarely ideal) solutions. We can now say that the measurement, benchmarking, forecasting and quantitative management techniques applied to property investments are comparable with other asset classes. If other problems are less fully resolved – the correct interpretation of valuation and price evidence, the relationship between the performance of unlisted and listed investment vehicles – advances in property research have at least put the ongoing debates onto a footing of solid evidence, and produced a clear formulation of the issues.

That position has been reached through many different strands of research – from academics, specialist commercial researchers and research-minded portfolio managers in different countries, not always easily communicated between those spheres. Much of it, indeed, remains private rather than public – confined to the top levels of major investors and their advisors. Having held senior positions in all those fields of research, Andrew Baum is singularly well qualified to draw the strands together into a coherent and accessible statement of the state of the art in applied property research. In a world swept by radical change – globalisation of investment markets, financial engineering of investment vehicles, the collection and dissemination of information – we can be sure that the state of the art will be transformed again over the coming decade. Here too the book offers a clear view of the next steps in the evolution of the industry, which will be read with keen interest by all those involved in it.

Tony Key
Research Director
Investment Property Databank
London, May 2000

Preface

This book is the result of the author's recently varied experience of applied property research, UK property fund management, international property investment and academic research. The many challenges and questions prompted by this varied experience have led to a varied set of thoughts and writings, some previously published and some not. The book is therefore something of a set of sketches. Nonetheless, they share a common subject matter, which can be described broadly as institutional investment in real estate, and a common foundation, broadly an international and capital markets context viewed with the perspective of a UK property professional.

The picture painted is of a major industry which is going through a period of rapid modernisation, facing more and more challenges as economies and markets become more global in character, as financial and investment markets become more and more creative, and as the world is swept by a wave of technological change. Creativity is at a premium, but at the same time this is an industry requiring – and developing – discipline, processes and measurement.

The text concentrates on UK institutional real estate, mainly retail, office and industrial, although residential is growing in importance as a UK sector and is included in the portfolios of most non-UK institutional investors. It is designed for practitioners facing the challenges described above, and those who may have to design solutions to tomorrow's problems. It is hoped that it provides a more straightforward and integrated view of the key issues in UK real estate than will be found elsewhere.

The book is divided into three sections. Part 1 provides a description of the market, the industry and the vehicles available, and a performance history of UK real estate as an asset class. Part 2 discusses the property investment process and the tools required to develop excellence in executing that process. Part 3 provides material for debate about the changes likely to take place over the short and medium term.

I am very grateful for the many fortunate partnerships which have made it possible for this material to be produced. Over the past decade, colleagues at the University of Reading, Prudential Portfolio Managers and at Real Estate Strategy, later Henderson Investors, have been responsible either for the better ideas or the more accurate analysis contained in these pages. In particular, I would like to thank Professors Neil Crosby, Colin Beardsley, Colin Lizieri and Charles Ward at Reading, John Partridge at RES/ Henderson, Paul McNamara at Prudential, and especially Andrew Schofield, Guy Morrell and Professor Bryan MacGregor with whom I was fortunate to work at both Prudential and RES/Henderson.

Andrew Schofield deserves particular mention. He was responsible for much of the analysis and some of the ideas in Chapters 3, 5 and 7, and our joint work at RES in the 1990s has influenced much of the book's content.

Tony Key has also allowed me to reproduce some of our joint work in Chapter 6, and Freeman Publishing has also allowed me to reproduce parts of my work with Peter Freeman for *Freeman's Guide to the Property Industry* in Chapters 1 and 2. Some of the ideas in Chapter 9 are based on the work of Charles Ward and Colin Beardsley, my colleagues in the property derivatives group. I am grateful to them all.

In addition, Tony Key of IPD and Richard Barkham of CB Hillier Parker acted as expert reviewers of the first draft of the text, and produced many suggestions for improvements. Tony Key proposed a much improved structure to the original book and Karen Baum acted as an expert copyeditor.

Any remaining errors are my own. In the text, he/his is meant to imply he or she/his or hers.

The place of real estate as an investable asset class is secure. The same cannot be said of existing vehicles, companies or managers, which and who will survive only through education, innovation and professionalism. I hope this small book makes at least a small contribution to their future success.

Andrew Baum
London
May 2000

List of Figures, Tables and Boxes

Boxes

The Author

Andrew Baum, chartered surveyor and investment analyst, is Professor of Land Management at the University of Reading and was until recently Director of International Property for Henderson Investors, London, England.

Formerly Property Research Manager for Prudential Portfolio Managers, managing director of consulting company Real Estate Strategy and CIO (Property) for Henderson, he is the author or co-author of several books and many papers.

At Henderson, he was responsible for the development of international real estate products, both public and private. The first Henderson international product, the Henderson French Property Fund, was launched in 1999.

As CIO at Henderson, he was responsible for the development of a branded investment process which emphasised Henderson's strength in research. This in turn derived from the Henderson purchase of Real Estate Strategy, a forecasting and strategic consulting business founded by Baum in 1990 and sold to Henderson in 1997.

He is a Fellow of the Royal Institution of Chartered Surveyors, a member of the Association of Investment Management and Research, the American and European Real Estate Societies, the American Urban Economics and Real Estate Association and the Society of Property Researchers. In 1999 he was elected Fellow of the Urban Land Institute.

From 1989 to 1996 he was a member of the board of the Investment Property Forum, and is currently co-chair of the Policy and Practice Committee for the Urban Land Institute in Europe and committee member of the Schroder Exempt Property Unit Trust.

He holds BSc, MPhil and PhD degrees from the University of Reading in the UK. He is the co-author of *The Income Approach to Property Valuation* (fourth edition, 1996), *Statutory Valuations* (third edition, 1997) and *Property Investment Appraisal* (second edition, 1995), and author of *Property Investment Depreciation and Obsolescence* (1991).

He is a member of the editorial board of *Real Estate Finance* (USA), the *Australian Land Economics Review*, the *Journal of Property Investment and Finance* (UK) and the *Journal of Valuation and Property Services* (Malaysia). He is also Editor in Chief of *Freeman's Guide to the Property Industry*.

Andrew Baum may be contacted by e-mail at: aeb@abaum.co.uk; a.e.baum@reading.ac.uk

PART 1

Real Estate: The Asset Class

Chapter 1

Introduction: Why Invest in Commercial Real Estate?

1.1 The importance of property investment

Real estate serves a vital function as shelter, or as what economists would call a factor of production. We need land to grow food; we need factory and warehouse space to make, store and distribute goods; we need shops to buy and sell those goods; and we need office space to administer and service those businesses.

Real estate or property (the terms are interchangeable) is also an asset class which is commonly found in the investment portfolios of global investors and the balance sheets of large corporations. Commercial real estate is used in this book to refer to shops, offices and industrial property: in the UK, the main examples of non-commercial property, residential property and agricultural land, are more commonly the preserve of the private investor.

In 1998, directly owned real estate accounted for some 6.7% of the value of the institutional investment market throughout the world (an estimate made by, among others, Prudential, a US insurance and financial services group). This represents a sum of US$1,241 bn. By adding the real estate owned by vehicles such as property companies in which institutions also invest and the property held as investments by private individuals, corporates and public sector bodies, this begins to appear to be a very important asset indeed.

The UK (with an estimated $170bn or £106bn) constituted around 29% of all European institutional real estate in 1998. In global terms, this represented 14% of global institutional real estate, the third largest share after the USA ($380bn, or 30%) and Japan ($217bn, or 17%). These are broad estimates and open to much interpretation, but they suggest the UK is a leading real estate market in international terms.

The London Business School has estimated the total value of all commercial property in the UK, including private investments, owner-occupied and government property and overseas ownerships, to exceed £250 bn. (This is broadly the universe from which the institutional estimate of £106 bn should be drawn.) The value of all residential property exceeds £1,000 bn. While the quoted property sector represents less than 2% of the market capitalisation of the London Stock Exchange, the institutional fund manager places more importance on commercial property.

The importance of the UK market in terms of its size is supported by the institutional and structured nature of the UK market. The professional organisation of property services is probably most recognised in the UK through the history and power of the Royal Institution of Chartered Surveyors and the global expansion of partnerships such as Jones Lang Wootton (now Jones Lang LaSalle) and Richard Ellis (now part of the Insignia group). In addition, the collection and analysis of ownership data is at its most developed in the UK, partly through the work of the Investment Property Databank, now an expanding global business. Finally, the City of London is the world's leading fund management centre (Baum and Lizieri, 2000), and this naturally adds to the importance of London as a centre for property investment and the services associated with it.

1.2 The sectors: principal characteristics

Commercial property risk and return characteristics vary from property to property and from sector to sector. What follows is a brief description of the qualities of the major UK sectors. (For more information, see *Freeman's Guide to the Property Industry*, from which this section is taken.)

1.2.1 Shop units

- There are over 500,000 shops in the UK and thousands of shopping parades. There are about 500 locations which attract a reasonable spread of multiple retailers. However, there are only 100–200 'prime' retail locations, typically with at least 100 shops each and minimum catchment populations of 50,000 plus.
- High street shop unit values typically range from £100,000 to £5 m and offer the potential for effective diversification.
- As single tenant investments they are straightforward to manage.
- They depreciate very little, as much of the value resides in the land.
- Supply is restricted by the importance of the location, so owners are protected from competition in many cases. Nonetheless, smaller high streets have suffered in recent years as shoppers

have sought greater shopping choice and convenience in out-of-town retail warehouses and shopping centres.

1.2.2 *Retail warehouses and parks*

- Highly popular with the price-conscious, time-poor, car-borne shopper in the 1990s, retail warehouses were the best performing sector for investors through most of the 1990s. Planning limitations usually restrict sales to bulk goods (DIY, furniture, carpets, white goods).
- Single units have lost popularity at the expense of retail parks typically of 75,000–150,000 sq ft (£10–30 m capital value). The few retail parks combining areas of 200,000 sq ft plus with open A1 (unrestricted retail) planning consents can become open-air shopping centres and command much higher rents. Rents in Fosse Park, Leicestershire, the most notable example, are now ten times the rate of stand-alone DIY units in many locations.
- Good parking and highway access are of vital importance.
- Recent poor performance may be explained by excessive buying pressure through the mid-1990s and general doubts about the retail sector in the midst of the e-commerce revolution.
- However, out-of-town retail planning consents have become increasingly difficult to obtain, supporting investor interest.

1.2.3 *Shopping centres*

- About 600 shopping centres have been built since the 1960s. They are mostly in town centres, typically providing 20–60 additional retail units. In-town shopping centre values range between £20 m and £100 m.
- The earlier shopping centres were often open to the elements. The later ones are in the main covered and climate controlled.
- A new generation of 1m sq ft centres such as the Metro Centre (Gateshead, outside Newcastle), Lakeside (M25 East of London, North of the Thames), Bluewater Park (M25 East of London, South of the Thames), Merry Hill (Birmingham) and Meadowhall (Sheffield), all on the edge of town, have all been successful and command values of £500–1,000m. All have superb road communications, creating enormous shopping catchment populations of 1m plus.
- Refurbishment, depreciation and service charges for common parts are big issues for shopping centre owners and their tenants.

- Specialist managers are necessary to manage the shopping mix and to extract full value from the centre; each centre is a major business in its own right.
- Because lot sizes can be as high as £1 bn, diversification is a challenge, although limited partnerships have recently taken a greater share of the market and offer some divisibility.

1.2.4 Offices and business parks

- Traditional town centre offices have been the worst performing UK property sector over 30 years.
- There is an enormous range of lot sizes. Outside London, only the biggest and best buildings are worth more than £20m. In Central London, there is a reasonably active market for lots of £100m plus.
- Depreciation and obsolescence have badly affected performance as occupiers' needs have changed and flexibility of layout and services has become the key issue. Many of the earlier buildings have been incapable of providing air-conditioning and raised floors for computer cabling.
- Some business parks have begun to command higher rents than town centre offices; time has yet to tell how robust this sector will be, but a movement towards the much higher levels of out-of-town or suburban offices common in the US is clearly under way.

1.2.5 Industrials and distribution warehouses

- Traditional industrial estates have historically performed best late in the cycle: strong performance following strong retail performance has been a typical pattern for the 1970s–1990s.
- Many older industrial buildings have shown surprising resilience to obsolescence and are still lettable several decades after construction.
- The perceived value of the industrial sector has increased with greater recognition of the lower risk to total returns associated with higher initial income.
- About 300 'high bay' distribution warehouses have been built in the last 15 years. They typically have floorplates of 100–300,000 sq ft and eaves heights of 12–25 m. They have attracted industrial investors because they offer reasonably large lot sizes (typically £5–25 m), new highly-specified buildings and tenants with good covenant strength.

- Distribution warehouses have generally failed to produce competitive total returns as low initial yields have combined with low levels of rental growth.
- Rents have been held down by just-in-time delivery methods and the resulting collapse in inventory levels, a ready supply of land outside the South East and the willingness of developers to work on narrow profit margins due partly to the abundance of pre-lets. This attitude is partly explained by the lack of speculative risk and the short period for which capital has been deployed.

1.2.6 Leisure schemes

- Leisure parks, normally anchored by a multi-screen cinema, a themed restaurant, a fast-food restaurant and a mixture of bowling, discotheque and other facilities, have become a popular investment in the 1990s.
- However, there are still less than 50 complete leisure parks and the schemes have been dominated by a handful of developers.
- Many funds have sought an exposure to the sector through co-investment vehicles and others are planned. Overall, however, the relative size of the sector makes it relatively unimportant.

1.3 The vehicles available for property investment

Several problems are associated with property investment. These include illiquidity, the bias of pension fund minimum solvency requirements against relatively illiquid assets, poor comparative returns during the 1980s and 1990s, and a lack of trust in property return indices (see Chapter 2).

An apparently obvious solution to many of these problems is the use of liquid traded property vehicles in place of the direct asset. A variety of legal structures exist which are capable of providing a means for investment in domestic or international real estate investment. In addition, much work is being expended in the development of new vehicles to provide this solution, with some indirect property media already in place, including property shares, property unit trusts and property index certificates.

Many countries have their own unique vehicles, such as the Australian listed property trust and the US real estate investment trust. These vehicles may have the primary objective of reducing tax, of achieving liquidity or of aligning the interests of the investors and the managers. They may exist to permit co-mingling

---

Box 1.1 After-tax returns on equity

Property cost	£2,000,000
Loan	£1,500,000
Tax on profits/gains	35%
Interest rate	7.00%
Growth	2.50%
Gross running yield	7.50%
Gross total return	10.00%
Return on equity after tax	12.35%

---

of investors, or may be special-purpose vehicles for the use of one investor acting alone. Their use has multiplied in recent years as a result of the continued search for liquidity and the success of REITs (see section 1.3.5 below), the increase in cross-border investment activity, often more attractive in a co-mingled format, and the generally more punitive impact of tax on foreign investors (but see College of Estate Management, 2000).

1.3.1 Special-purpose corporate vehicles

The company is a popular format for the ownership of both domestic and international property. Its prime advantage is to allow complete flexibility in the size and quantity of the number of investors in the vehicle; in addition, it introduces the possibility of liquidity if the vehicle is offered in the public markets. In the UK, however, tax is paid on the capital gains made by UK companies and on the profits made by these companies. In addition, tax is paid by shareholders on the dividends distributed by companies, so the conversion of freehold ownership into a corporate structure introduces an extra layer of tax (College of Estate Management, 2000).

This is more of a problem for taxpayers, typically overseas owners or private individuals and corporates, than it is for institutional investors. However, international institutions may be caught in this net.

The most common means of addressing this disadvantage is to reduce double income tax as far as possible by minimising profits and dividends. This is most commonly achieved by introducing borrowing, so that the interest charge will be set against rental income to reduce annual profit. This may have the added advantage, depending on the relationship between interest rates and running yields, of introducing a positive leverage or gearing effect, so that returns to equity after tax may exceed total returns on the vehicle as a whole after tax and even in some cases before tax (see Box 1.1).

A second means of reducing income tax is to introduce equity in the form of debt. This can be achieved by issuing investors with loan notes instead of, or alongside, share certificates. Tax on interest received may then be treated differently.

Established offshore, corporate vehicles can be highly tax-efficient and hence attract international investors. Companies set up in the Channel Islands, for example, can sell property free of all UK capital gains tax. For this reason and others, the UK is seen to some extent as a tax haven for international investors.

Fee structures in such corporate vehicles, modelled on US private equity (venture capital) funds, typically attempt to align the interests of investor and manager by rewarding the manager on a performance basis. The manager may typically charge a base fee calculated as a percentage of the value of the assets managed, and additionally take a proportion (say 20%) of the total return over a minimum hurdle (say 15%).

Much international property investment utilises this type of vehicle. It raises some interesting questions. A UK life fund may typically consider this type of vehicle in allocating cash to international property investment. Its decision may be based on the returns available after tax on equity, compared to the gross returns available in their domestic market. Its domestic investments are unlikely to be geared, and the false comparison of similar returns on low-risk domestic investment and high-risk, highly geared or levered international investment may be tempted.

1.3.2 *Property company shares*

Over the longest time series available, property companies have outperformed direct property investment by around one and a half per cent each year. Both have significantly underperformed the UK equity market.

The volatility of property company shares has, however, been much higher than that of the direct property market. On an annual basis, the standard deviation of returns has been only 12% on direct property compared to 37% on property company shares.

In addition, the performance of property company shares has not mirrored that of direct property. The correlation of return between direct property and property company shares has been only 20% compared to a correlation between property company shares and the UK equity market of 60%. In other words, UK property company shares look like equities, and a poor substitute for direct UK property.

These relationships are not fixed: the results of any analysis are subject to the time period used. For example, the relationship between property company shares and the UK equity market was very strong in the 1970s while the relationship between property company shares and the direct property market has been stronger since 1980. (See Chapter 9 for more details about the usefulness of property shares as a diversifier.)

1.3.3 Property unit trusts

Many smaller professional investors use what are known as collective investment schemes or co-mingled funds. Typically managed by fund managers, these are pooled funds which allow smaller insurance companies and pension funds to achieve diversification without the high fixed costs and illiquidity of holding direct property. The main type of pooled fund is the property unit trust.

Property unit trusts are the main vehicle used by pension funds to gain access to diversified portfolios of UK real estate in a form which allows replication of direct market performance characteristics. They are unlisted, the unit prices are determined by valuations, and liquidity is limited to a small amount of secondary market trading activity and the guarantee that managers will buy and sell units, albeit at spreads which replicate the cost of buying and selling direct property. The largest example of the UK pooled fund, the Schroder Exempt Property Unit Trust, manages (at May 2000) over £1.1 bn of commercial property assets for more than 600 different corporate pension fund unit holders.

Property unit trusts are tax free for qualifying pension funds. While they have to invest in domestic property to protect this status, they can be established offshore to appeal to international investors. In addition, specialist unit trusts are increasingly being established. Leicester's Fosse Park, the highest rent out-of-town

Table 1.1 Total return and standard deviation: direct property and property unit trusts, 1979–94

	Return %	*Risk* %
Direct property	11.1	9.8
Property unit trusts	11.8	8.3

Source: IPD/Watson Wyatt Worldwide

retail park in the UK, is held in an offshore property unit trust vehicle for the benefit of a mix of domestic and international investors.

The investment performance of property unit trusts has been similar to that of direct property. For example, between 1979 and 1994 the total return on direct property was 11.1% each year. The total return on property unit trusts compared favourably at 11.8%, and their risk was slightly lower (see Table 1.1). The absence of large Central London offices from most unit trusts in the early 1990s, when these assets severely underperformed the market, explains a large part of this.

The correlation between property unit trusts and the direct property market over this period was higher than 90%.

There is a small secondary market dealing with the transfer of units on a matched bargain basis, so that the liquidity of the property unit trust market may be a little better than the liquidity of direct property, but liquidity is still limited by three factors. Firstly, the current property unit trust market is only worth around £5 bn, 5% of the direct institutional market. Secondly, property unit trust managers typically only trade on a quarterly basis. Thirdly, property units are ultimately as illiquid as the underlying asset.

The open-ended nature of property unit trusts means that investors can deal directly with the manager rather than with each other through a secondary market. This can be problematic in rising and falling markets. Flows of capital into and out of the vehicle can create greater difficulties for the manager than rising and falling share or unit prices would create for the managers of a closed ended vehicle such as a property company.

Particular difficulties were evidenced in 1990–93, when net sales of units led to forced sales of property, damaging the performance of some unit trusts. This in turn led to more investors wishing to exit, forcing further sales of units and then forcing sales of properties in a vicious downward spiral.

In strong markets, intense performance pressure can be placed on managers by net inflows of cash. Managers are forced into a position where they wish to invest quickly, but only in attractively priced assets.

Despite the problems caused by the open-ended structure, property unit trusts remain popular. In general they behave like direct property. Liquidity is not significantly better than for direct property, but property unit trusts are ideal for small funds due primarily to the professional management and diversification benefits of a pooled vehicle.

1.3.4 Limited partnerships

The limited partnership structure is unregulated and simpler to operate than the unit trust. It has recently been successful in attracting investors, usually into specialist or single property investments. Limited partnerships are tax neutral or tax transparent vehicles – meaning that the vehicle itself does not attract taxation and partners are treated exactly as if they owned the assets of the limited partnership directly. This creates an enormous advantage for the vehicle, which has become increasingly popular in the UK for co-mingled property ownership.

Over £5bn was invested in limited partnerships in the 1997–99 period alone. The ownership of Bluewater Park, for example, a £1 bn shopping centre developed by Lend Lease, was converted to a limited partnership in 1998 and partnership shares sold to investors.

The main disadvantages are limited liquidity, with stakes tradable only on a matched bargain basis, and limited ownership spread, with only 20 first-level partners allowed. It is possible that this limitation may be removed at some point, and limited partnerships may even become tradable on the stock exchange. If these two changes were to happen, this vehicle may become enormously popular and a true revolution in UK property ownership would then be set in train, similar to the real estate investment trust (REIT) revolution in the US.

1.3.5 Real estate investment trusts

The US real estate investment trust is a tax-transparent, quoted vehicle which is forced to distribute the majority of its earnings and to limit its gearing. This provides the features which many would look for in the ideal property vehicle, providing pure property performance features in a liquid form. Its growth in the 1990s from a total market capitalisation of around $8 bn to something over $175 bn demonstrates this view.

This appears at first sight to be the perfect liquid property vehicle, but the issue is discussed in more detail in Chapters 8 and 9.

1.3.6 *Property index certificates*

Property index certificates, launched by Barclays in the mid-1990s, are derivative investments whose buyers are provided with synthetic returns matching the annual return on the IPD annual index. As in the gilt or bond market, the buyer pays a capital sum which is either par value or a price representing a premium or discount to par depending on demand in the market.

The issuer provides a quarterly-in-arrear income based on (but not exactly the same as) the IPD annual income return, and following expiry the par value is repaid together with a large proportion, but not all, of the capital appreciation in the IPD index.

While performance is directly linked to the capital performance of the IPD annual universe, under normal circumstances property index certificates lock in marginal underperformance of the IPD annual index due to the management costs charged. Correlation with the direct market is nonetheless very high, and in a multi-asset or international context these instruments provide the pure diversification benefits of UK property. However, liquidity is low due to the small size of market and the lack of a true secondary market.

Derivatives are dealt with in more detail in Chapter 9.

1.4 International real estate investment: old and new styles

It is common to find simplistic assertions that international real estate investment will provide effective diversification for pension plans. This model, which assumes an investor objective defined in terms of expected return and the standard deviation of expected return, is highly flawed, both because it fails to recognise the diversity of real investor objectives and because there are many costs of international diversification which are unrecognised in the measure. While diversification fails to explain a very large proportion of current international real estate investment, it explains much of the activity of the 1970s and 1980s.

Two new styles of international real estate investment vehicle have emerged in the 1990s, driving much of the recent international activity. The first is the transfer of real estate ownership into venture capital or private equity format. The second is investment in property share funds.

1.4.1 Private equity funds

These are special purpose vehicles, usually in a corporate format and often involving complicated cross-border structures. They are always closed ended and usually limited life co-mingled funds.

This type of investment vehicle was commonly used for domestic investment in the US in the 1980s. For many reasons the format became largely discredited, but the access provided to difficult markets for foreign investors, tax efficiency and a lack of alternatives have all helped to overcome resistance to the vehicle.

This is now a popular medium for international property investment. The returns advertised are high, usually in excess of 15% on equity. It can be purpose-made and therefore tax-effective for certain investor domiciles and types. Gearing is common, at levels up to 60–80%, both for performance and tax purposes. The fund manager often has an investment alongside clients and includes a performance element in the fee charged.

This vehicle has carried much of the 1990s US investment in markets such as Poland, Thailand and China. While there are many flaws in this investment format – the limited life format and its lack of liquidity being two – its main advantage is that it clearly accesses the diversification potential of private real estate.

1.4.2 Securitisation

Securitisation may result in the longer-term possibility that real estate investment becomes either venture capital in its riskier form or an industry sector in its developed form. The UK has been no exception in its development of securitised and other indirect forms of property ownership. The packaging of listed securities into funds which provide exposure to a country's property sector, or to a region or a sector, is likely to gather pace. The growth of property share benchmarks such as those provided by Salomon Smith Barney and Global Property Research and the development of global and regional property share funds (Jupiter, Henderson, ABN-AMRO) are signs of a maturing market.

However, for the supply of property share funds to grow requires growth in the number and size of listed property companies. In 2000, market pressure in the UK was operating in the opposite direction, as large discounts of share price to net asset value made it more attractive to take property companies into private ownership and exploit the property values in other ownership formats the performance of which is not linked to the stock market.

1.5 Commercial property owners

Insurance companies, pension funds and other investing institutions hold over £90 bn, or around four times the aggregate value of the quoted property sector, in commercial property as part of their investment portfolios – typically 3–10% of their total assets. They have gained importance over recent decades at the expense of the traditional property owner.

1.5.1 Decline of traditional owners

The structure of ownership (or, more accurately, control) of UK commercial property has been changing in both obvious and subtle ways over the last 25 years. First, the combined forces of privatisation and globalisation have had their intended and inevitable impact. The traditional owners – the great private landed estates, such as the Church, the Crown, the Oxbridge Colleges, central and local government – have, as a whole, lost relative influence, while overseas owners have increased their presence. To take an example, the overseas ownership of City of London office buildings increased from around 3–5% to 20–25% over the period from 1972 to 1998 (Baum and Lizieri, 1999), while the proportion owned by the City Corporation and the Worshipful Companies fell markedly.

1.5.2 Increased role of fund managers

Second, there has been a less apparent shift in management away from the insurance companies and pension funds which were so dominant in 1980, when property made up as much as 22% and 12% respectively of their total assets, towards fund managers and property companies (the distinctions between which are becoming increasingly blurred). Through the 1980s the institutional investor dominated the higher levels of the industry, controlling the larger transaction business and (in collaboration with chartered surveying businesses) driving best practice and forming industry lobbies such as the Investment Property Forum. In the 1990s the effects of privatisation and outsourcing reached down to the institutions. There has recently been a restructuring of their investment and property divisions, with the result that the power base now lies within specialist fund management operations, which may themselves be owned by what used to be insurance companies and are now financial services groups.

1.5.3 Changes in the surveyor's role

These developments have produced a proliferation of vehicles, a more complex industry structure and a confusion of ownership and management. The traditional UK property service providers, the chartered surveying partnerships, have been severely challenged by these changes. While (prior to the recent explosion of Internet-based property listing services) there has been no serious threat to the transaction-based business of the traditional surveyor/agent, investment management is another story. First, fund managers can access large sums of capital for business development or for co-investment in large blocks of property alongside clients, which traditional partnerships cannot do. Second, the Financial Services Act of 1986 imposed discipline on the securities businesses of financial services groups. While the regulations do not apply to property, they nonetheless suggested the possibility of unmanaged conflicts of interest among the traditional service providers, which may earn the majority of their fees from transaction business while acting as investment managers.

Even so, many of these businesses have been successful in maintaining their own fund management operations by creating their own 'Chinese walls' (Jones Lang LaSalle, for example, now being a top three property fund manager by assets under management, separately branded as LaSalle Investment Management). Some now have access to significant capital, but this has been at the cost of their independence. An epidemic of takeovers in the mid-1990s resulted in the sale or merger of many of the most respected chartered surveyors to or with US-based real estate businesses. As examples, Jones Lang Wootton merged with LaSalle, Richard Ellis and St Quintin were sold to Insignia, Hillier Parker was sold to Coldwell Banker, and Healey & Baker was sold to Cushman & Wakefield.

1.5.4 Property companies

Property companies have been successful at surviving two severe challenges to their very existence, in 1973–75 and in 1991–93. In both property recessions many famous property companies became insolvent and disappeared. While the extremely strong performance of the stock market in the 1980s and again since 1993, coupled with a growing demand for liquid (easily traded) property investment vehicles, has provided some support to the albeit poorly performing share prices of the survivors, its weighting as a proportion of the stock market has declined significantly since 1989. Nonetheless, the property company sector includes well over 100 companies and the largest UK property owner of all, Land Securities, is a FTSE 100 company.

1.5.5 Overseas owners

Over the last 15 years the UK, alongside the US, has been one of the few countries capable of attracting a wide range of overseas property investors. Most have been particularly attracted to the City office market, home to more international banks than anywhere else in the world. The City property stock was almost wholly domestically owned until Big Bang in the mid-1980s, after which successive waves of Japanese, American and German capital have taken levels of overseas ownership from 2% to something approaching 25% (Baum and Lizieri, 1999). London is a major international property market, and the financial services output of the City accounts for some 5% of UK GDP; the importance of the City property market alone to the national economy is substantial.

The category of overseas owners includes property companies, US-based real estate investment trusts (REITs), insurance companies, pension funds, German open-ended funds and others. They are almost certain to continue their recent expansion into the UK commercial property market. The more committed participants in recent years have included:

- the German open-ended investment funds (for example, CGI, DESPA, DEGI and DIFA);
- German insurance companies and pension funds;
- pension funds and property companies from the Netherlands (for example, ABP, PGGM, Rodamco and Wereldhave);
- sovereign investors such as the Abu Dhabi Investment Authority and the Government of Singapore Investment Corporation;

- US-based funds looking for international diversification and/or higher returns at the riskier or development ends of the UK market (for example, Blackstone and Security Capital).

The historic compartmentalisation of real estate into domestic property markets is unlikely to continue for long (see Chapters 7 and 8). The City of London office market provides an excellent example (Baum and Lizieri, 1999).

1.6 Current challenges

For the purposes of this book, the importance of real estate lies in the fact that it has been one of three major asset classes which insurance companies and pension funds like to invest in, either directly or through property shares, which are increasingly accepted as a major sector of the global stock market. The cult of equity has dominated western investment strategy in the 1980s and 1990s to the extent that equities now dominate most institutional portfolios, especially in the US, the UK and Hong Kong. On the other hand, in Germany and some other continental European countries, bonds have always been the largest component of the mixed asset portfolio. In either case, property is treated as the third asset class – and often a very poor third.

UK institutions, for example, held over 20% of their investments in real estate in 1980. The average is now around 6%. There are two reasons for the decline. First, the returns on property relative to equities have been low, so that the allocations to equities have increased as a result of the unmatchable growth in the capital values of equity portfolios. Second, the positive performance characteristics of property, traditionally seen as reasonable return, low risk and a good diversifier, have been challenged.

The experience of property investors in the early 1990s was enough to persuade many of them that it was time to abandon the asset class. Several property companies became bankrupt; many banks developed severe shortfalls in their loan books through exposure to property loans; many householders found they owed more than they had borrowed by developing negative equity; and, worst of all, it became acutely apparent that the liquidity of property was not the same as the liquidity of equities and bonds. Perhaps property owners did not reduce their asking prices quickly enough; certainly it takes longer and costs more to sell property.

Because of this, the investment market is clearly pondering the potential for global *securitisation* of real estate. Property companies in the UK are neither sufficiently tax-efficient nor appropriately regulated to provide a securitised real estate product capable of being offered to institutional and retail markets. But over the period 1990–98 real estate investment trusts in the USA and authorised property trusts in Australia each saw explosive growth in markets where the legal and regulatory framework permits privately held real estate assets to be transferred into tax-efficient public vehicles. The UK and other markets seem to be poised for a similar revolution.

In addition, the search for return has led to *globalisation*, meaning a transfer of attention from domestic investors and investments to international investors and assets. At the same time, it has promoted sector *specialisation*, as a single-country focus by investment managers has been supplemented by single sector (such as distribution) multinational focus. Increasingly, profits will gravitate to those providers of space which create market niches characterised by excellence of service and a standardised product. This is already evident in shopping centres, retail warehousing and serviced offices; more niches will follow. The providers will eventually expand beyond national boundaries, like Coca-Cola and McDonald's, in order to exploit their comparative advantage.

1.7 Conclusions

Whatever the future format of real estate investment vehicles, the generic case for investing in real estate will need to continue to be made. This is dealt with in Chapter 2.

The traditional form of institutional real estate investment is direct investment in property portfolios. Globalisation and the associated changes have added two new formats: private equity vehicles and investments in co-mingled and securitised funds. Globalisation and pension fund growth mean that rapid growth is expected in all areas of international real estate activity. The UK will be no exception to this. Rationalisation is inevitable as scale of operation becomes vital, and excellence in management will be key. This is dealt with in Part 2 of this book.

Growth and concentration is set to continue. Venture capital/private equity funds will continue to capture pension fund investment as the international real estate investment industry moves from emerging, through developing, to maturing. The industry sector will grow as a proportion of global stock markets and attract more recognition, more index funds and more investment share funds. Whether the traditional property advisor will capture market share is less clear. Whatever the future holds, it is likely to continue to be rich in challenges for the global property industry. These challenges are dealt with specifically in Part 3 of this book.

Chapter 2

Why Invest in Real Estate?

2.1 Property as an asset class

Since 1980, insurance companies have reduced their property holdings from allocations as high as 20% or so to the current level of around 6%. This fall in property weightings can be attributed to several factors. These include:

- the operational difficulties of holding property, including illiquidity, lumpiness and the difficulties involved in aligning the property and securities management processes;
- high weightings at the end of the 1970s boosted by ten good performance years for real estate and ten poor years for equities, coupled with poor comparative returns during the 1980s and 1990s;
- the introduction of new alternative asset classes, some offering the income security and diversification benefits associated with real estate, including index-linked gilts and overseas securities;
- a lack of trust in property data, due to the nature of valuations, suspicions of smoothing in valuation-based indices and the lack of long runs of high-frequency return histories; and
- the bias of pension fund minimum solvency requirements (Pensions Act 1996) against relatively illiquid assets (see Investment Property Forum, 1995).

The result has been a mismatch between the importance of the asset class in value terms and its current weighting in institutional portfolios. It is arguable that the case for property may have been overstated in the past, or alternatively that misunderstandings and suspicion regarding the asset class have reduced its appeal to institutions.

The recent history of property investment in the UK is dealt with further in section 2.10.

2.2 What makes property different?

History also shows that property is a true third asset, distinctly

21

Box 2.1 Depreciation and its impact

The extremes of performance are illustrated by the following two office properties in the City of London.

21 Great Winchester Street, a building of 18,000 square feet which in 1986 was 16 years past a major refurbishment, was valued at that time at £386 per square foot. The ERV was £24; the yield at which a sale might be expected following a new letting was estimated at 6.5%.

Token House, at 8–10 Telegraph Street, a 17,000 square feet building having undergone a major refurbishment in 1985, was valued at that time at £673 per square foot, with an ERV of £32 and a yield of 4.75%. In terms of underlying value (in other words, ignoring the impact of lease contracts), it was worth *roughly double* the value of 21 Great Winchester Street per unit of space.

In 1996, 26 years since refurbishment, 21 Great Winchester Street was valued at £19.50, at 7% and at £278 per square foot. This was a decline in capital value of £107 or 28%. Seventy-two per cent of its underlying 1986 value remained, and it had declined in value at the same rate as the market (3%). Ageing had not therefore severely affected the underlying value of the building.

In 1996, 11 years old and just past its second review, Token House was worth £133 per square foot, valued at £10 and 7.5%. *It was now worth less than half the value of the comparison.* It had fallen in value by £540 per square foot, or no less than 80% of its underlying 1986 value: 20% of that value remained. It had suffered depreciation of 18% each year, of which perhaps 3% can be blamed on the market.

---

different from equities and bonds, for three demonstrable reasons. First, it is, unlike equities and gilts, a physical asset. This means it is subject to deterioration and obsolescence, and needs regular management and maintenance. Physical deterioration and functional and aesthetic obsolescence go together to create depreciation, defined as a fall in value relative to an index of values of new buildings (see Box 2.1). The problem of building depreciation or obsolescence of freehold buildings should not, as has usually been the case in the property world, be understated. Poorly designed buildings located in low land value areas will produce a more rapid fall-off in performance than carefully restored and refurbished buildings in the City of London. A failure to distinguish between these vastly different investment types is very dangerous. The office sector failed to outperform the IPD universe in every year except two since 1981: this was probably one of the major causes.

Second, unlike equities, property's income stream is governed by very long contracts, and, unlike gilts, the income from a freehold is both perpetual and may be expected to increase at rent reviews and change at lease ends. Property's cash flow and investment character flow from the effects of the customary occupancy lease, supported by statute and case law (see Baum and Sams, 1997).

Third, the supply side of property is regulated by local and central government. The control of supply complicates the way in which an economic event is translated into return. A loosening of policy, such as happened in the mid-1980s, created the conditions for an immediate building boom and a subsequent crash.

However, like all assets, the performance of property is ultimately linked to some extent to the performance of the economy and the capital markets. The economy is the basic driver of occupier demand, and, in the long term, investment returns are produced by occupiers who pay rent. However, in the shorter term – say up to ten years – returns are much more likely to be explained by reference to changes in required returns or yields. Required returns do not exist in a property vacuum but are instead driven by available or expected returns in other asset classes. As these move, so should required returns for property and property prices.

As all investment managers are required to state, good returns in the past are no guide to returns in the future. Simple extrapolation is dangerous because the economy is changing all the time. Understanding the linkages is increasingly necessary for the property professional. Most commentators and investment practitioners believe there is some form of property 'cycle', which is a useful way of thinking about these linkages (see section 2.11).

2.3 Relative returns

Property is usually described as a low to medium risk asset. Its returns should therefore be expected to lie between those produced

Box 2.2 Illustrative returns available on equities, bonds and property

Year	Equities	Property	Bonds
0	−100.00	−100.00	−100.00
1	3.00	6.00	6.00
2	3.23	6.00	6.00
3	3.47	6.00	6.00
4	3.73	6.00	6.00
5	4.01	6.00	6.00
6	4.31	7.30	6.00
7	4.63	7.30	6.00
8	4.98	7.30	6.00
9	5.35	7.30	6.00
10	197.48	128.19	106.00
IRR	10%	8%	6%

Notes:
1. The equity is bought with an initial dividend yield of 3%; the initial yield on the property is 6%; the bond has a running yield of 6%.
2. Dividend growth for the equity is a constant (and demanding) 7.5%; the property's rental growth begins at 4% but slows to 2% after the first review as the building tires and depreciates.
3. The property capitalisation rate or yield increases by 1% over the ten-year holding period, while the equity yield stays constant.

by equities and those produced by bonds. The risk of property has certainly been lower than the risk of the equity market and this low risk has to some extent offset low delivered returns.

The uncertainty of the nominal dividend income produced by an equity over the holding period compares with the absolute certainty of nominal income produced by a fixed-interest security held to redemption. Commercial property falls somewhere between the two in terms of certainty of income. In a standard lease, with upward-only rent reviews, the initial rental income set at the start of a lease remains certain, with only the uplifts expected at each rent review being uncertain. Given long leases, the principal return to the investor is an income return, and the value of the reversion at the expiry of the lease (while largely uncertain) is of reduced importance. Overall, therefore, commercial property should be a low to medium risk asset compared to bonds at the least risky end of the spectrum and equities at the most risky.

To explore this, we can set up a theoretical return model. Box 2.2 shows the returns that would be generated by the three asset classes under a set of plausible assumptions. A 6% ten-year bond bought at par will produce 6% if held to redemption; an equity producing an initial return of 3% with dividends rising at around 7% will produce 10%, fairly reflecting the higher risk in equities and the lower risk in gilts. Under these conditions, which are arguably rosy for equities and neutral for bonds, it can be shown that property can be expected to generate a return midway between those of bonds and equities.

2.4 The investment context

Nonetheless, in the last 25 years it has been the property market's fate to disappoint institutional investors who might have allocated their cash elsewhere: to fixed-interest securities (gilts, both conventional fixed-interest and index-linked, and corporate bonds) or to equities (UK or international).

Strong bond returns in the 1990s (produced by a drop in interest rates and inflation) and unprecedented high returns by equities in the 1980s and 1990s have resulted in UK commercial property underperforming government bonds, and underperforming equities by more than would be expected.

A comparison of the annual total returns on the three main UK asset classes (equities, fixed interest gilts and property) over an 18-year period, using geometric mean returns, shows that equities out-performed property by nearly 8% each year, and gilts outperformed property by almost 2.5% (see Table 2.1). Investing in property would not appear to have been optimal over this period.

These are not encouraging statistics. The future, however, is unlikely to be – indeed, should not be – like the immediate past. For reassurance, we can question the sustainability of the conditions of the recent past from which the empirical results are derived. The conditions of the 1980s and 1990s may have been the worst possible for property relative to bonds and equities. The deregulation of planning brought about by the Thatcher government, coupled with

Table 2.1 UK asset total returns, 1981–99

Year	Property	Property shares	Equities	Gilts
1981	15.0	4.8	13.6	1.8
1982	7.5	−5.2	28.5	51.3
1983	7.6	35.1	28.8	15.9
1984	8.6	23.5	31.8	6.8
1985	8.3	11.6	20.2	11.0
1986	11.1	24.8	27.3	11.0
1987	25.8	23.7	8.7	16.3
1988	29.7	27.8	11.5	9.4
1989	15.4	5.3	35.5	5.9
1990	−8.4	−18.1	−9.6	5.6
1991	−3.2	−13.5	20.8	18.9
1992	−1.7	−12.6	19.8	18.4
1993	20	89.1	27.5	28.8
1994	12	−18.6	−5.9	−11.3
1995	3.5	6.9	23.0	19.0
1996	10	28.0	15.9	7.7
1997	16.8	24.6	23.6	19.4
1998	11.8	−21.9	13.7	25.0
1999	14.5	16.5	23.8	−3.5
Average	10.38	9.72	18.26	12.84

Notes: averages are geometric means; gilts are benchmark ten-year redemption yields; equities are FT all share dividend yields; property is IPD annual universe, standing investments; property shares are FTA real estate.

Source: IPD, Datastream

consistently overestimated but falling inflation rates and the cult of equity have arguably provided one-off shocks to property's relative performance.

2.5 Debt-enhanced returns

The history of ungeared direct returns disguises the returns that have been available to investors' equity over most sub-periods of the last 25 years. Just as home-owners can, in times of rising house prices and low interest rates, significantly enhance the return on the cash they invest by borrowing, property companies and private commercial property investors use debt finance to increase returns on equity. By using rents to pay interest and partial capital repayments, investors can enjoy a tax-efficient net cash flow and return on their equity investment well in excess of the reported total return available to whole-equity investors such as insurance companies (see Chapter 8). These 'geared' returns are rarely reported but explain most private capital investments in UK property.

2.6 The benefits of asset class diversification

Mathematical models based on modern portfolio theory (MPT) play an important role in the investment market, especially in the advice on investment strategy and asset allocation given by actuaries and consultants to pension funds and insurance companies.

MPT reflects the desire of investors to achieve higher returns, low individual asset risks and a smooth return on the entire portfolio. Asset allocation advice has, since the acceptance of MPT, traditionally required a view on three values: the likely future return on an asset class; its risk (usually defined as volatility and measured in units of standard deviation of return over a given period); and its correlation with other asset classes. This last factor measures the extent to which upward and downward movements in the values of two variables are linked together.

MPT has both led to, and has been further encouraged by, the development of asset allocation models. Strong prospective returns, coupled with low standard deviation of returns and a low correlation with equities and gilts, would provide a very strong argument for holding an asset.

When assets are combined in a portfolio, the expected return of a portfolio is the weighted average of the expected returns of the component assets. However, unless the assets are perfectly correlated, the risk is not the weighted average: it is determined by the correlations of the component assets. The way in which assets covary is central to portfolio risk, as low covariance produces diversification opportunities.

Jones Lang LaSalle provides the longest available run of consistent annual data describing the performance of a reasonably well diversified portfolio of real properties. The results show the following:

• property returns have been below the return on equities but competitive with the return on gilts;

Box 2.3 Return and volatility

Year	Property A	Property B
1	10	20
2	10	20
3	10	−40
4	10	25
5	10	25
Average	10	10
Standard deviation	0.00	28.06

- property volatility has been less than the volatility of both equities and gilts; and
- property has been much less well correlated with equities and gilts than equities and gilts have been correlated with each other; in other words, while equities and gilts have usually performed well or badly at the same time, property has outperformed or under-performed at different times, thus smoothing out the overall performance of a portfolio with assets of all three classes.

This suggests that property offers portfolio risk reduction to holders of bonds and equities.

Smoothing, however, is a large problem colouring this data. In some years property yields do not appear to change, and it is clear that this can be the result of a scarcity of transaction evidence and the behaviour of valuers rather than a steadily performing market.

2.7 Volatility, valuations and liquidity

Return is one side of the coin; risk is the other. For most investment professionals, including the actuary working with a pension fund or life company, the measurement of risk rests on the concept of volatility rather than the layman's concept of the probability of a potential loss. Volatility is the fluctuation of returns around an average return. For example, one property (A) might show a 10% return each year for five years (see Box 2.3). Over the five-year period it would have shown 0% volatility as the actual return in each year was the same as the average return. If another property (B) had shown a positive return of 20% for the first two years, followed by a negative return of 40% in the third year and two further years of a positive return of 25%, it would have produced the same average return of 10% per annum. However, the volatility in returns would have been much greater. This is usually measured in units of standard deviation. This is a measure of the average distance of each observation or data item from the mean of that data.

The total returns delivered by commercial property over the period 1972–99 have been less volatile even than the returns from gilts. This appears to suggest that property has the lowest risk, but this conclusion is flawed. Low volatility of delivered nominal returns disguises the illiquidity (or lack of easy or regular sale) of property, which introduces a risk not reflected in the volatility of notional returns based solely on valuations from period to period. In addition, valuation-based returns are themselves believed to be biased towards lower volatility than typical underlying market conditions support. There are several reasons for this.

Valuers are thought to be naturally cautious about preparing valuations reflecting the absolute peaks and troughs of the market. A valuation bias is commonly introduced by the use of dated comparable evidence. In addition, index construction methods introduce temporal averaging, as the date of year-end valuation may be spread over quite a period.

Less obviously, this problem also affects the correlation numbers. It can be argued that the property correlations are lower than they should be, for the same reason that the correlation between a series of random numbers in one column and a fixed value in the other will tend towards zero. The greater the fixity of the property return series – the greater the amount of smoothing or serial correlation – the greater will be the tendency of the correlation of that series with returns in efficient markets to be close to zero. Note that the values for the correlations of property returns against equity and gilt returns are both around 0.1.

So three indicators are needed for assessing the appropriate weight of property in a multi-asset portfolio, two of which present two large problems. Standard deviations of returns from year to year understate true property risk, and correlations between property and the other assets may be unreliable. For this reason, various efforts have been made by academics to improve the position, which usually imply the use of statistical techniques to adjust the data (see, for example, Brown and Matysiak, 2000). To date, this effort has largely been ignored by practitioners.

2.8 Liability matching

For many investors, particularly pension funds which have liabilities linked to future wage levels, the need to achieve gains in money value (in nominal terms) is of less concern than the need to achieve gains in the purchasing power of assets held (in real terms). Again, property might be viewed as a medium real risk asset. The cash flow might (although subject to deterioration and obsolescence) be expected to increase in line with inflation over a long period, but in the short term rent is also subject to the constraint imposed by five-yearly rent reviews. This means that in the short run the income produced is of a fixed-interest nature and hence prone to damage by inflation. This is not true of equities, but is even more true of conventional (not indexed) bonds.

Short-term inflation is, of course, less of a concern for the investor with long-term liabilities. In addition, year on year correlations between the asset classes may be said to be of limited interest to pension funds and insurance funds with longer-term liabilities. They are more likely to be concerned with their ability to match liabilities (wage inflation linked pensions or nominally fixed endowment mortgages) without increasing the contribution rate of the employer or employee, or to declare a bonus.

A more interesting measure for long-term investors might therefore be the coincidence of good or bad returns on different asset classes over longer periods. It is then possible to judge whether the poor correlation between property and equities is merely the result of valuation lags or smoothing, or alternatively whether there is something more fundamentally different about the way the assets perform. An analysis of long-term returns suggests that the best and worst periods of performance for property have not coincided with those periods for bonds and equities, and that property offers long-term advantages for investors with long-term liabilities (see Chapter 9).

2.9 Benchmarking

Financial services organisations, like other businesses, concentrate on market share as one of the ways to grow profits. Like any business, they are also concerned with the performance of their competitors and business risk. To prove that they are delivering value as fund managers, there is a requirement for measuring return relative to a competitor benchmark. The property fund manager is

---

Box 2.4 Excess returns and tracking error

Year	Index	A	B	A excess	B excess
1	18	10	20	–8	2
2	17	10	20	–7	3
3	–30	10	–40	40	–10
4	20	10	25	–10	5
5	21	10	25	–11	4
Average	9.2	10	10	0.8	0.8
SD	21.97	0.00	28.06	21.97	6.14

---

therefore concerned not only with absolute return, but also with return relative to a performance benchmark such as IPD. Similarly, the multi-asset manager is encouraged to invest in property simply to reduce the risk of performing differently from competitors with a property weighting.

The danger to fund managers departing from standard weightings is demonstrated graphically by two high-profile examples. In 1998–99, PDFM lost the mandate to manage many billions of pounds of client money after reducing its stock market holdings in the mistaken expectation of a fall in share prices. In 1999, Mercury Asset Management was sued by the Unilever Pension Fund after reducing weightings in certain key shares, resulting in below-average returns.

Box 2.4 shows how the fund manager views risk. Absolute volatility, as measured by standard deviations, shows manager B to be much worse than manager A. However, this is of less concern than the riskiness of excess returns (returns delivered relative to an index or benchmark). The standard deviation (SD) of return relative to the index is called tracking error.

In the table, manager A has no volatility, but the index does. Hence the returns achieved by A relative to the index (Aexcess) are volatile. They are in addition more volatile than the excess returns, or the tracking error, on B. Manager B produced more volatile returns, but they were more in line with the market and probably introduced less business risk for manager B than manager A, who would have been uncomfortable in all years except year 3.

2.10 A UK property performance history

2.10.1 1950–73: from low inflation to a boom

In the right market conditions, banks have been willing to lend more against the security of property than against other assets such as equities. This is a result of property's income security and the land, bricks and mortar salvage value of a non-performing property loan. In turn, the availability of debt has attracted a large number of private investors and developers to property. In the 1950s and 1960s, the reconstruction of Britain characterised by slum clearance, comprehensive development schemes and new towns, coupled with the ready availability of long-term mortgages at low rates of interest, enabled developers like Hyams, Clore, Land Securities and Hammerson to develop and hold major portfolios. Rapid increases in value in the 1960s, partly fuelled by growing rates of inflation and partly by the long postwar boom, went straight into the pockets of equity owners in these companies whose borrowing costs were often fixed. At the same time some possibly ill-judged government restrictions on development – such as Office Development Permits – held back supply and drove up real rents.

Insurance companies had, up to the mid-1980s, been market participants as long-term mortgage lenders and as owner-occupiers or lessees of office space. Having observed the equity gains that were being made by borrowers, they began to consider exposing their own cash to the expected increasing value of property. By this route insurance companies became equity investors in property as well as investors in property-backed, fixed-interest debt. More purchasers in the market added to pressure for higher prices.

The 1960s property boom was an indication of the end of the low inflation period, and the end of low fixed-interest rates. Inflation also introduced the necessity for regular and increasingly more frequent rent reviews (see Baum and Crosby, 1995). The typical shop lease in 1960, for example, was for 21 years without rent review. Between 1962 and 1971 rent review clauses were inserted in 62% of all new leases. Between 1965 and 1970 the normal rent review term was seven or 14 years. After the Barber Boom (the loose money boom of the early 1970s presided over by the Heath government's Chancellor of the Exchequer, Anthony Barber) and the consequent inflation of 1971–74, five-yearly rent reviews became typical. In the mid-1970s there was even an attempt to move the market to three-yearly reviews. The market has since settled on five years as an acceptable compromise between lessor and lessee.

Table 2.2 City office rents, nominal and real, 1950–2000

Year	Nominal rent (£ per sq ft pa)	Inflation index	Real rent (£ per sq ft pa)
1960	£1.38	100.00	£1.38
1965	£4.75	119.04	£3.99
1970	£12.88	148.84	£8.65
1975	£13.50	274.46	£4.92
1980	£23.50	536.87	£4.38
1985	£36.38	759.76	£4.79
1990	£50.00	1013.01	£4.94
1995	£35.00	1197.27	£2.92
2000	£50.00	1361.04[e]	£3.67[e]

e = estimate

Source: Henderson Investors, Datastream

2.10.2 1974–81: a small cycle, high inflation

The conversion of property from a vehicle for fixed interest investment to an equity play for institutional investors was consolidated in the aftermath of the Barber Boom and the oil crisis of 1973. Loose economic policy drove a boom and, together with the rapid rise in oil prices, a subsequent crash in UK property markets, the equity market and the economy as a whole. As a result of this very serious economic shock, many property companies and several secondary banks became insolvent, many on the back of injudicious property lending, and the government was forced into the organised degearing of property companies in its so-called 'lifebelt' operation.

Commercial property found its way into insurance company portfolios at this time as borrowers defaulted on mortgage repayments. At the same time, property was available from distressed property companies at low prices, and the asset looked attractive as an inflation hedge, as retail prices, chased by wage increases (supported by powerful trade unions), oil prices and loose monetary policy, leapt upwards at annual rates of 25% or more. Following a famous meeting at the Prudential, a group of insurance companies entered the weak equity and property markets in 1975 en masse. For a time, rents almost kept pace with inflation, taking City rents from a low of £135 per sq m (£13.50 per sq ft) to a high of £235 (£23.50), despite limited real growth and demand (see Table 2.2).

2.10.3 1981–90: high inflation, another boom

By 1980 around 20% of all insurance company assets and 10% of pension fund monies were invested in commercial property, which then embarked on a protracted period of underperformance relative to the UK stock market. Pushed on by the Thatcher government's campaigns for business, privatisation and enterprise at the expense of the welfare state, equity portfolios increased in value much more quickly than property portfolios – partly to be expected, partly not – so that more of the institutions' new money was invested in equities than in property. The result of outperformance by equities and the greater allocation of new money to that sector was a reduction in property weighting between 1980 and 1999 to the present averages of 5–6% for pension funds and 7–8% for insurance companies.

This period included a cycle in property values dramatic enough to rival or even exceed the boom and bust of 1972–5. Big Bang and the economic boom of 1986–89, when consumer expenditure growth reached levels as high as 6% a year, produced huge levels of bank liquidity. The apparent security of property for lenders, burned by their experience of Third World debt, again enabled property companies to increase their borrowings – and financial gearing – to capture the fruits of another property boom. Residential owner-occupiers geared up and many bought second homes. According to DTZ (1999a), bank lending to property reached all-time record levels (see Table 2.3).

In the downswing, the pattern of 1972–75 was repeated. Interest rates rose, property rents fell and capital values fell by even more. An economic downturn led to tenant defaults; borrowers were unable to cover interest by rent received, and their debt often exceeded the total value of the properties they owned. Properties were sold at huge discounts to their previous values. Negative equity affected new homeowners and property companies alike, in the latter case usually leading to liquidation. Between summer 1990 and summer 1994 around 15 quoted property companies, many previously glamorous and successful such as Olympia & York, Mountleigh, Rosehaugh and Speyhawk, became insolvent, putting such prominent schemes as Canary Wharf and Broadgate in the hands of bankers. Innumerable smaller property companies were also taken over by receivers. The resulting property crash and its accompanying economic recession were both, by some measures, the most severe of the twentieth century.

Table 2.3 Bank lending to property, 1981–99

Year	Nominal lending £bn	Inflation	Real lending £bn
1981	5.5	100	5.50
1983	8.5	113.60	7.48
1985	12.5	126.49	9.88
1987	22.0	136.23	16.15
1989	44.6	154.07	28.95
1991	48.5	178.54	27.16
1993	39.8	188.10	21.16
1995	33.8	199.33	16.96
1997	35.1	210.60	16.67
1999	45.1	214.40	20.35

Source: DTZ, Bank of England

2.10.4 1990–99: deep recession, low inflation and globalisation

While the 1960s and 1980s property markets were dominated by debt-driven property companies, and the 1970s was the decade during which the equity capital of institutional investors became dominant for the first time, the 1990s was the decade during which the international property owner emerged as a long-term player in the UK property market. In the same way that UK institutions replaced bank lenders as sources of capital and took advantage of weak prices and a demoralised property market in 1975, German capital entered the UK market in 1993 at a time of distressed lenders and weak prices but of relatively positive fundamentals.

By late 1992, the UK economy had been in recession for 18 months. The property market was suffering a disastrous slump. The oversupply of London offices created through the boom of the mid to late 1980s, coupled with very weak tenant demand and rents which had crashed from their 1989 real peak, created a potent mixture. Property companies had been squeezed by interest rate rises in the late 1980s, by a scarcity of debt following the record levels of lending by banks, and by a fall in investor demand for property. When rents started to tumble in 1991 the final piece of the jigsaw was in place, and the UK saw property company failures, non-performing bank loans and a loss of investor confidence.

In late 1992, the UK withdrew from the European Exchange Rate Mechanism. As a result, interest rates fell, gilt yields fell and sterling was effectively devalued against the German mark. This marked a turn in investor sentiment. A London office building might have been worth only 50 per cent of its 1989 peak. Rents appeared to be approaching a floor. Yields were at an all-time high – both in absolute terms and relative to gilts and equities. There were many office properties in central London which had been let at initial rents as high as £65 per square foot in 1988 and 1989 but whose market rents were now only a fraction of that figure.

For these over-rented buildings the rent due to the landlord was likely to continue unchanged for a very long time as a result of upward-only rent reviews. In some cases market rents were not expected to regain the original rent set before the end of the lease, as nominal and real growth forecasts were both very bearish at the time. In 1992, some analysts were forecasting further falls in nominal rents with no recovery until 1996 – a reasonably accurate view, as it turned out – and inflation levels of around 4%. This was a low level in the context of the 1970s and 1980s, but an over-estimate in retrospect. Hence many over-rented buildings continued to feature in portfolios as late as 2000.

Investors were now able to buy a fixed income secured on property with the prospect of an equity conversion at some time – perhaps distant – in the future. Overseas purchasers, especially Dutch and German funds, could now purchase investments very like those they were familiar with – fixed-income low-risk bonds – at very attractive yields relative both to their domestic bonds and to UK gilts, whose yields fell from roughly 8.5% to 6.5% during 1993 (see Table 2.4). Not only that, but sterling's devaluation meant that a larger building could now be purchased by an overseas investor for the same outlay in their domestic currency terms, improving both the comfort factor of the deal and the investment gains associated with any future currency appreciation.

The economy was emerging from recession and expectations were already shifting toward the rent rises that materialised in 1995–96. High returns resulted from a dramatic yield shift in late 1993 and early 1994, followed by the steady albeit undramatic recovery of rents. The sea change in the market heralded a new wave of property company flotations: Chelsfield, Argent, Rugby and Pillar all floated in this period, cashing in on the dramatic increase in their net worth caused by the combination of high gearing and increased capital values.

Table 2.4 Five-year cost of borrowing and ten year gilt yields, 1960–99

	Five-year swap	*Ten-year gilts*	*Base rate*
1986	n/a	10.65	11.00
1987	9.84	9.68	8.50
1988	11.365	9.96	13.00
1989	12.37	10.26	15.00
1990	11.665	10.95	14.00
1991	10.35	9.73	10.50
1992	7.87	8.26	7.00
1993	5.88	6.10	5.50
1994	8.915	8.71	6.25
1995	7.06	7.42	6.50
1996	7.63	7.51	6.00
1997	6.86	6.29	7.25
1998	5.43	4.36	6.25

Source: Datastream

Steady progress was made in the 1996–2000 period, as rental growth became widely established in all sectors and lower gilt yields enabled property yields to fall. While double-digit returns were produced every year by the property market, market overheating was never a serious threat. Investors continued to pay more attention to equities, and in particular technology stocks, so that equities continued to outperform property, albeit with increasing dispersion at the individual stock level. While new economy stocks produced enormous returns, old economy stocks disappointed, and equity portfolios began to look more dependent on smaller numbers of high-value technology stocks and hence more risky. (In 1998 in Finland, the market ex-Nokia fell, but the market as whole produced 72% returns. As a result, Nokia rose in value to the point where it represented more than 50% of the capitalization of the Hex (the Helsinki stock exchange).)

By contrast, the property market of early 2000 appeared in many ways to be well balanced, with debt, equity and international capital all apparently comfortable with its exposure to a steadily performing and stable market. Low inflation, low interest rates and a steadily growing economy produced returns of around 12% and 15% each year in 1998 and 1999, showing real price rises of 3–6%, and very high returns to geared equity investors (see Table 2.5).

Table 2.5 IPD total returns, inflation and GDP growth, 1971–99

Year	IPD return	Inflation rate	IPD real return	GDP growth
1981	15.0	12.0	2.7	−1.3
1982	7.5	5.4	2.0	1.8
1983	7.6	5.3	2.2	3.7
1984	8.6	4.6	3.8	2.4
1985	8.3	5.7	2.5	3.8
1986	11.1	9.7	1.3	4.2
1987	25.8	3.7	21.3	4.4
1988	29.7	6.8	21.4	5.2
1989	15.4	7.7	7.1	2.1
1990	−8.4	9.3	−16.2	0.6
1991	−3.2	4.5	−7.4	−1.5
1992	−1.7	2.6	−4.2	0.1
1993	20	1.9	17.8	2.3
1994	12	2.9	8.8	4.4
1995	3.5	3.2	0.3	2.8
1996	10	2.5	7.3	2.6
1997	16.8	3.6	12.7	3.5
1998	11.8	2.8	8.8	2.2
1999	14.5	1.8	12.5	2.1

Source: IPD, Datastream

Limited oversupply of property and speculative development left the market in better shape than it had been ten years earlier. Expected stable five-year returns of 10–15% were the consensus view at the beginning of the year 2000. Some turbulence is nonetheless likely, as history teaches us that the one certainty is change, the occasional violent shock is normal in financial and capital markets, and developers never turn down the offer of a bank loan.

2.11 Evidence of cycles in the UK commercial real estate market

It has been suggested (MacGregor, 1994) that repeatable patterns, or cycles, can be seen in the history of development, occupier and investment markets. These are expressed in the form of developments, rents and yields, with these in turn driving capital values and returns.

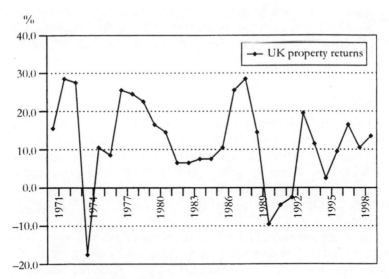

Figure 2.1 UK property returns, 1971–99

Figure 2.1 illustrates what many would describe as a cycle in UK property returns over the period 1971 to 1999.

2.11.1 Developments

The inelasticity of property supply in response to price changes is perhaps the most important variable which explains the existence of a cycle of supply, rents, capital values and returns. Empirically, a 4–5 year cycle in property development is apparent, but this is not coincident with the rent cycle. Development activity appears to be highly pro-cyclical with GDP growth and property values (rising and falling at the same time), but exhibits sharper rises and falls.

Current development profits have been a good explanatory variable of development activity. There is a strong relationship between office development and changes in rents, suggesting a degree of adaptive behaviour among lenders, investors and developers with a tendency to follow the market, often in an exaggerated fashion. A period of excessive optimism is followed by a period of excessive pessimism. Adaptive behaviour can explain much of the late 1980s boom and bust development cycle. As prices rise, prices are more likely to be expected to continue to rise; development profits are a function of continued price rises; hence price rises lead to ever-increasing supply levels, which create the conditions for lower prices (disaster myopia). The time lag between the inception and completion of developments creates an inevitable supply cycle.

2.11.2 Rents

Rents have also been strongly pro-cyclical with GDP. Barras (1994) shows how periods of growth in GDP above the long-term trend rate of growth have been coincident with periods of growth in rents above long-term trend growth. The demand side is pro-cyclical with economic growth indicators, but inelasticity of supply means that even highly regular demand cycles can generate irregular rental cycles.

Barras identified short cycles (4–5 years, the classic business cycle operating on occupier demand), long cycles (9–10 years, a tendency for severe over-supply in one cycle to feed part of the next demand cycle), long swings (20 years, associated with major phases of urban development) and long waves (50 years, technology-based).

2.11.3 Yields and capital values

There is no clear relationship between yields on UK property and other asset and money market yields and rates. The fairly flat pattern of UK property yields in the recent past, for example, has been accompanied by a continued decline in gilt yields. Evidence of cyclicality around a flat trend may be discernible over a long period.

The flatness of yields results in an extremely strong relationship between rental growth and capital value growth, both strongly pro-cyclical, although some extreme market movements have been strongly yield-driven (examples include 1993–94 and 1973–74).

2.11.4 Returns

There is some relationship between returns and the business cycle, but this is less strong than the relationship between changes in rents, capital values and economic growth simply because income returns have been reasonably stable from period to period, thereby reducing the sensitivity of total returns to economic growth variables. A 4–5 year cycle in the rate of all-property return has been observable.

Recent work by IPD (IPD, 1999, drawing on historic data for Scott, 1998) provides the fullest picture of long-term UK performance yet available. Data assembled from various sources covering the period 1921 to 1998 shows 16 'fairly distinct' peaks and troughs in the market. IPD identify six completed cycles, with peaks in 1925–28, 1935, 1950, 1954, 1960–64, 1973, 1979–81 and 1989. They suggest that those cycles have ranged in length from four to 12 years, with an average of eight years; upswings have run from two to seven years, and downswings from two to nine years.

These 'recurrent but irregular' patterns are not necessarily the result of a single cyclical process. They could be the product of overlapping cycles of different lengths (five and nine years). It is tempting to see a shorter cycle as demand-driven, linked to the business cycle in the economy, and a longer one as supply-driven, linked to slower fluctuations in new development.

The property cycle is linked to the economic cycle, but the precise nature of the relationship varies from one cycle to another. These property cycles appear to be clearer in form than equity and bond cycles and more exaggerated in effect than economic cycles. Why might this be the case?

2.11.5 Cycles: the result of market inefficiency?

Bjorklund and Soderburg (1997) suggested that autocorrelation (previous upward movements in prices leading to increases in prices in the next period) affects real estate returns to the point that a speculative bubble can be proven to have formed. Antwi and Henneberry (1995) identified what they called habit-persistent (another term might be adaptive) behaviour by lenders and developers.

Wheaton (1999) suggests that forward-looking (rational) expectations by agents lead to stability, while myopic (adaptive) behaviour promotes oscillations – or cycles.

Grenadier (1995) examined the way owners of space will restrict supply in an upswing. Letting space at a market rent on a five-year lease involves the giving up of a five-year American option (the right to call a higher rent at any time). In an autocorrelated occupier/rental market, it is easy to see how letting at the market rent may appear to be a suboptimal financial decision, especially when the supply side is so slow to respond to demand and price. Withholding space in this way exaggerates the supply shortage and the cyclical upswing. (It may also lead to empty space in a downswing: the well-known case of Centre Point in London is a good example.)

These concepts indicate inefficiency in real estate markets. They affect the way space is developed, the way rents are agreed for space and the way prices are paid for real estate investments. They exaggerate and elongate upturns and downturns, and create the appearance of definable cycles in real estate markets. Sticky prices affect occupier, investor and developer markets, elongating and exaggerating real estate cycles.

Rates of change in rental values and vacancy rates are slow, due to the actions of intermediaries or agents and the costs of moving. Occupiers have to take account of the cost of moving in bidding for new space. Intermediaries, in the form of real estate brokers, tend to smoothe rental value fluctuations by relying on historic comparable evidence in assessing new market rent levels. Development cycles are slow to reverse due to the commitment created by the large amounts of sunk (human and physical) capital required to complete a project.

Rates of return are also autocorrelated, due to valuation smoothing. This goes some way to support conventional views of the low volatility of real estate returns and the poor correlation of property with the main asset markets.

2.12 Conclusions

The past can be used to suggest many things, both factual and false. It would clearly be incorrect to assume that history will repeat itself, following a standard pattern. Nonetheless, data can be used to show that property markets, both occupier and investor markets, clearly respond to economic cycles and economic events. Property advisers certainly need to understand these linkages, and the way market inefficiencies serve to exaggerate or disguise the impact of the economy and the capital markets on commercial property performance.

The UK 'cycle' of the 1990s was sufficiently different in its shape (a gradual recovery of values and activity, interrupted by the sharp value rise driven by falls in the gilt yield in 1993–94) to prompt commentators to suggest that cycles are a thing of the past. Better, or wiser, management, better market information, better management and pricing of the debt supply have all been suggested as reasons why this may be the case. An alternative view is that cycles are an inherent feature of property performance, and that (while they may appear in different forms and may not be perfectly predictable) some evidence of property cyclicality will always emerge.

Whether or not the future will be characterised by cycles, efforts to anticipate economic and property market change are essential in the property investment process. This process is dealt with in Part 2 of this book.

PART 2

Managing Performance

Chapter 3

The Management of Commercial Real Estate

3.1 Introduction to portfolio management

Property investment managers in the UK have traditionally been proud of their skill in the selection and asset management of the individual building. Until the 1980s property portfolios tended to be seen as simple aggregations of individual buildings. There was little reference to portfolio theory in practice or in university courses, and little was made of the linkages between the property market and the macro economy or the capital markets. This has changed, and with it the emphasis has shifted from property and asset management to portfolio and fund management. At the same time, changes in the structure of the industry and pressures to outsource have created a new facilities management industry.

We have already made use of five different management terms, which we need to define.

- *Fund management* is the administration of a pool of capital, with the intention of investing the majority or all of the capital in a group of assets. Hence a property fund may have some cash, or utilise gearing.
- *Portfolio management* is the administration of the property assets within the fund, not including the cash or gearing, but taking account of the structure of the portfolio as a whole. All or part of this function could be subcontracted by a fund manager to a property specialist. Sales and purchases might be left to the discretion of the portfolio manager (a discretionary appointment) subject to net inflows or outflows of cash imposed by the fund manager or client.
- *Asset management* is the administration of the property assets within the fund, not including the cash or gearing, and not taking account of the structure of the portfolio as a whole, but with the objective of maximising financial performance of each property asset for the client. All of this function might naturally be subcontracted by a fund manager to a property specialist. Sales and purchases might require the approval of the fund manager.

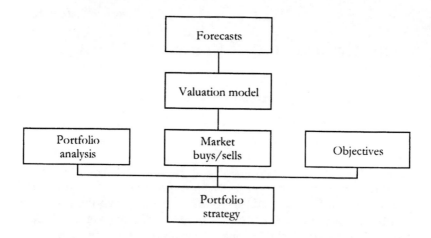

Figure 3.1 The investment process

If this is the case, the appointment might be said to be advisory rather than discretionary.

- *Property management* is the administration of the property assets, not necessarily with the objective of maximising financial performance for the client beyond the efficient and prompt collection and payment of rent and service charges. The objective of the property manager might instead be to offer satisfaction to the user of the assets, the occupier or customer. This distinction explains the rising popularity of *facilities management*, a wholly and more comprehensive user-oriented approach to property management, sometimes called corporate real estate management.

More recently, a strategic approach has become popular in property portfolio management. This involves consideration of the structure of the portfolio relative to a benchmark, forecasts of return and risk for the portfolio, often top down by property type or location, and a strategy which involves buying and selling. The investment process which has become more typical in the UK property investment management business is shown in Figure 3.1.

Commonly, forecasts of rental growth and yield movement are applied at the market, sector, region, city and property level. These, fed through a discounted cash flow valuation model (see Chapter

4), will suggest market buys and sells – those sectors, towns and buildings where the returns on offer, as estimated by the investment manager, exceed the risk-adjusted required return.

A valuation model is simply a way of comparing the expected or forecast return with the required return (the risk-adjusted cost of capital) or, equivalently, the correct initial yield with the current market yield. The inputs into a valuation model are the investor's views on rental growth, depreciation and risk. These are used to establish the correct yield or the expected return. This is compared with the current market yield or the required return to establish whether the asset is correctly priced, underpriced or overpriced. This produces market buy and sell decisions.

Deciding whether assets or markets look cheap is not sufficient to determine a portfolio strategy. The current portfolio structure is also significant, and a portfolio analysis will be undertaken to identify where the manager is underweight or overweight relative to a given benchmark. In addition, the manager's or trustees' objectives must be taken into account in determining what action needs to be taken. That action will be prescribed in the form of a business plan or portfolio strategy.

3.2 Practical portfolio management

This section covers some general aspects of property portfolio management and focuses on active portfolio management. It starts from three basic propositions.

1 *Investment strategies are like business plans.* They should be driven by a clearly stated and understood objective. They should take account of the fund's strengths, weaknesses, opportunities and threats (or constraints). They should be reviewed using a form of performance appraisal.
2 *There are three ways to achieve performance objectives.* These are: managing portfolio structure; positive stock selection and successful negotiation of transactions; and active management of the properties within the portfolio.
3 *The necessary technology includes three sets of models, all of which can add value.* These are: models used to produce forecasts; valuation models, which operate at all levels for the market down to the individual building; and portfolio models, used to control risk and assist in the optimisation of portfolio planning.

3.3 Business planning and fund strategy

Developing a strategy for the management of a portfolio is rather like producing a business plan. This includes the following processes:

1 *A clear statement of objectives.* The manager needs to know what he is trying to achieve and when. This should include a statement of required return, risk tolerance and timescale. Return and risk are likely to be relative to a benchmark. This process is analogous to the agreement of a mission statement.

2 *Strengths, weaknesses and constraints.* A portfolio analysis is a statement of where the fund is now which is needed to be able to establish realistic objectives. Stock characteristics, market conditions, expected flows of cash and staffing can be regarded as constraints on the fund achieving its objectives.

3 *The strategy statement.* This is the business plan. How is the objective to be achieved, and by when?

4 *Performance appraisal.* How well did we do? Did we achieve the objective? Are there any other standards of performance we should make reference to?

It needs to be recognised that more than one set of interests needs to be considered when adopting a mission and writing a business plan. The organisation may have several, sometimes conflicting, objectives. In an investment management organisation, these are all likely to relate to risk and return, a common means of measuring which are the mean and variance of annual total return. Mean-variance analysis, albeit simplistic in the context of a large and complex organisation, is useful, because:

- it is a commonly accepted theoretical foundation for investment and finance;
- it reflects the motivations of some actors in the business, for example some fund trustees and some research economists;
- it is most easily referenced in finance and investment publications and it is commonly taught.

However, it is not a useful way of defining the mission of most fund management organisations. Funds or managers will be concerned with other things.

The practical issues facing most investment managers are to do with long-term survival. This concentrates the mind on liabilities and solvency, which requires the advice of actuaries. Will the asset income stream be sufficient to pay the annual liabilities of the insurance or pension fund?

It also concentrates the outlook on profits or market share. As in any business, managers should be concerned with competitors and business risk. This leads to the pinpointing of return relative to a competitor benchmark.

3.4 Setting investment objectives

There are three possible performance objectives for an investment portfolio. First, it may have a simple target of maximum return or profit: this should, but may not, be subject to an understanding of the risk that might be accepted in the pursuit of that target. Second, it may have a set of liabilities to meet. These may include interest payments for a property company portfolio, annuities and bonuses for a life fund or pension payments for a pension fund. These are both appropriate objectives for managers to pursue for the benefit of the client investor. Third, it may have relative performance objectives. These are commonly in place but are primarily in place for the benefit of the manager.

Typically the property portfolio will be only one part of a larger fund. It is therefore unlikely there will be any consideration of liabilities at the property level: if liabilities are considered explicitly, it will be at the multi-asset level. Consequently return maximisation is the most common objective type, and because business endeavours are typically competitive, the performance objective is almost always set relative to a market or benchmark measure.

Several criteria should determine the precise framing of the performance objective. These will have an impact on the return target and risk tolerance, the benchmark adopted and the timescale over which performance is measured.

3.4.1 Criteria

Objectives should be achievable yet testing. They should be marketable, in other words capable of attracting investors. They must be testable, so that performance measurement is capable of determining success or failure. This should then be capable of leading to a reward of some sort (performance fee, bonus). Finally, the objective must be specific in terms of risk control.

3.4.2 Return and risk

The return objective will typically be expressed relative to the

Table 3.1 WM percentile rankings, 1994 total returns (%)

	95th	Median	5th	Range
Property	3.0	13.0	20.8	17.8
UK equities	−8.4	−5.8	−2.3	6.1
Gilts	−12.4	−9.6	−5.1	7.3
Overseas equities	−9.9	−5.4	−2.3	7.6

Source: World Markets

benchmark. It could be to achieve average performance, to achieve above median performance, to achieve 2% (or any other number) above average, or to achieve upper quartile performance; or it might represent a variation of any of these.

The return objective should be realistic when considered against the current structure of the portfolio, possible restructuring and transaction costs, staff levels and other constraints.

Any investment carries risk and there is a trade-off between return and risk. Thus the higher is the required return, the higher is the risk to be taken. If the manager seeks to achieve top quartile performance, he must take a higher risk of achieving lower quartile performance than if the objective is median performance. Risk tolerance should be made explicit.

Because information is relatively scarce, properties are heterogeneous and there is no central marketplace, property is traded in a relatively inefficient market. As a result, it is arguably easier to outperform the index by sector structure and by stock selection than it is in the securities markets. Considerable data exists to enable this potential to be measured.

The opportunity to add value is illustrated by Table 3.1, which shows the range of returns that managers of various asset classes achieved in 1994. It illustrates the enormous range associated with property.

3.4.3 Benchmarks

It is unlikely that a fund will want to make decisions without any knowledge of the portfolios and strategies of its competitors: to do so would create a business risk. However, it is not possible to construct an index fund in property because each building is unique.

For the property market, it is possible to obtain information from IPD on specified subsets of the databank such as large pension funds, but not on individual named funds. More typically trustees will set the IPD average return as a benchmark: that is the most widely accepted view of the market. This has the advantage of convenience but can cause problems for some fund managers if the type of fund they manage differs greatly from the IPD average.

Approximately 33% of the total IPD universe comprises the eight largest life funds. In 1990, large life funds had 10% more in offices (Central London), 6% less in retail and 4% less in industrials. This caused large problems for life funds in the following years.

Performance differentials between large and small funds are inevitable for a number of reasons.

- Larger funds can gain access to large lot size markets such as London offices. This can be good (1986–88) or bad (1991–93).
- The impact of stock-specific characteristics may be smaller in a large fund because of greater opportunities to diversify.
- Larger funds can undertake developments, which can produce high returns but which are typically riskier.

For example, large life funds outperformed the IPD average by 0.9% on average each year during the period 1981–88. Occupational pension funds underperformed the IPD average by 1.3% on average each year during the same period. In simple terms, London offices and developments and active asset management were positive performers over that period, and pension schemes had less access to these sectors and activities.

Cash and liquidity will also be an issue. How does the benchmark deal with this? There are significant differences in this respect between IPD, which to date has ignored cash and gearing, and standard property unit trust measures (for example, Combined Actuarial Performance Services (CAPS) which measures unit price performance where unit prices are affected by cash and gearing levels).

3.4.4 Time horizons

It is unrealistic to expect returns of 2% above average every single year. The level is testing and such consistency is nearly impossible: 1–1.5% above median has typically been sufficient to produce upper quartile performance. In addition, there is always property-specific risk, including valuation timing, to be considered. Funds are valued at the year end, but in practice between November and

January. In a rising or falling market this timing difference can be of great importance. It is more realistic to set a target in terms of three- or five-year averages: the effects of valuation timing, illiquidity and specific risk are then reduced.

This should be made very clear: the performance objective is increasingly the criterion by which the fund manager will be judged both as organisation and individual.

3.5 Strengths, weaknesses, constraints: portfolio analysis

There are three broad parts to the portfolio analysis. These are:

- an analysis of recent performance;
- a statement of current portfolio structure; and
- an assessment of the strengths, weaknesses and constraints affecting the organisation.

3.5.1 Recent performance

Fund manager appointments in property are most commonly made subject to a three-year or five-year review. The performance objective may be framed in these terms. Whether or not this is the case, the manager's strategy will be influence by his recent performance. There will be times when greater risks are encouraged to recover lost ground; there will be other times when the appropriate strategy will be designed to lock in the fruits of good past performance by eliminating tracking error from the portfolio.

3.5.2 Current portfolio structure

In either case, it is necessary to examine the structure of the portfolio relative to the chosen benchmark. While the region is a highly dubious unit of analysis (see Table 3.2 below) this is typically done by sector/region. These sector/region combinations are the asset classes: they are groups of properties which are thought to be affected by the same broad economic factors. In the current market, over-renting is also an important aspect of structure.

If the portfolio structure is identical to the benchmark, the only risk remaining relative to the benchmark is specific to individual buildings rather than systematic. This could be diversified away by having a large number of buildings, although in practice this is rarely possible because of costs and lot size.

The analysis of structure identifies those sector/regions in which the fund has an above- or below-average representation relative to the benchmark. This analysis is combined with forecasts of the sector/regions. If the fund has less than the benchmark in a sector/region which does well, the fund will perform below average. If the fund has more than the benchmark in a sector/region which does poorly, the fund will also perform below average.

Thus, an analysis of the structure of the fund relative to the benchmark is crucial: when taken together with market forecasts and the fund objectives, it will suggest sector/region combinations to buy or sell.

3.5.3 Strengths, weaknesses, constraints

It is not wise to determine the fund's ideal objective without considering how easy it is to achieve. It has to be implemented and that implementation will lead to performance measures and rewards.

Implementation may be helped or hindered by a number of factors. A number have already been covered. Others include the following.

- The scope for changing the shape of a fund will depend on new money coming in or money being withdrawn. Cash inflows can create opportunities to change the fund shape or apply capital to active management. Cash outflows can create enormous pressures on performance, especially in an illiquid market.
- It is also necessary to consider practicalities: whether it will be possible to undertake the proposed level of sales and purchases in a sensible time. This is a particular concern in inactive or small markets and for large funds.
- Particularly for small funds, there may be stock-specific factors which mean that the required sales cannot or should not be made.
- The cost of sales and purchases should be included in the analysis.
- The impact of taxation needs to be considered for some vehicles.
- For small funds, it may not be possible to gain exposure to large value markets with large lot sizes such as the London office market.
- The fund may not have the necessary expertise in-house and may require external agents.
- The timing of any change in strategy and changes in tactics is important: it is necessary to anticipate market movements and to buy and sell at the most advantageous moments.

3.6 Structure and stock selection

The most commonly accepted way of summarising the skills available to a property fund manager is to separate the production of outperformance from portfolio structure from the performance produced by stock selection. This is covered in more detail in Chapter 4.

3.6.1 *Structure*

In considering a plan for altering the structure of a portfolio, relevant issues include the appropriateness or otherwise of sector/region classifications, the accuracy and value of forecasts and portfolio size as it impinges upon the manager's freedom to balance the portfolio across three sectors, five sectors or 10 or 50 sector/regions.

This will also be affected by research staff size and expertise and by the culture of the organisation, which may or may not have valuable views and processes applied to other asset classes (for example, gilts).

3.6.2 *Stock selection*

Forecasts and portfolio analysis help to identify the sector/regions in which to buy. This provides a basis for stock selection: the buying and selling of individual properties. It focuses the work of those who have to identify actual buildings to buy or sell. The traditional way was to look for 'good' buildings, however defined and regardless of the impact on structure and consequent return and risk. However, an investment which appears 'good' in its own right need not be good in a portfolio context.

Forecasts may also be available at the town level and will direct sales and purchases. Other analyses may suggest subsectors in which to buy or sell, and identify features such as size, age and so on. Another important consideration is minimum and maximum lot size. It is then up to the surveyors to find and select underpriced stock.

For small portfolios, it is essential to look at the individual buildings in the portfolio when considering strategy.

Research (Morrell, 1993) also suggests the impact of uneven lot sizes has a major impact on the risk of many portfolios. This is because the direct property market is characterised by assets which are both heterogeneous and indivisible. The ability of many

Stock selection skills	Market forecasting ability	
	Good	Poor
Good	Concentrate on underpriced stocks	Concentrate on underpriced stocks
	Shift sector weights based on forcasts	Hold market weights
Poor	Diversify	Diversify
	Shift sector weights based on forcasts	Hold market weights

Figure 3.2 Passive and active strategies

portfolios to diversify away specific risk by holding many assets is often limited because a relatively small number of properties often account for a large proportion of the fund by value.

Indeed, for most funds, strategy is best considered iteratively, taking account of stock factors and constraints. There may be some particular feature of a property which means it should be sold or not sold despite the sector/region weighting. Examples include potential marriage value, development potential, refurbishment potential, lease structures which need to be changed before sale and so on. This is less of a problem for large portfolios: the impact of any one property is not likely to be significant in a £5 bn portfolio.

Active stock selection will require appropriate staff size, organisation and reward structure. Organisations do not always recognise the obvious implications of Figure 3.2.

3.7 Indexed portfolios and tilts

It is natural for managers to attempt to reduce risk by matching the sector/region composition of an index. At the same time, managers may believe in their ability to spot underpricing in property types – for example, secondary or high yield property. In equity fund management, this is called style management.

This risk control with a style bias can also be called tilting the portfolio. This involves creating a bias within an asset class. Thus a fund could hold the benchmark proportion for the asset class but select particular types within the class. Examples in equities would include concentrating on the shares of small electronics companies within the electronics sector; a property example would be to concentrate on shopping centres within the retail sector, or, as above, concentrating on secondary investments. For more on this topic, see Chapter 5.

3.8 Using forecasts and valuation models

At the national (UK) level it is possible to build econometric models linking rental growth in each sector to the main macroeconomic variables which influence rents and to changes in supply. It is possible but a little more difficult to do this at the regional level; it is also necessary to have a view at the town level, but this is the most difficult to construct by using purely econometric methods.

Rental growth forecasts are inputs into the valuation model but high rental growth is absolutely no guarantee of good performance. If all investors expected high rental growth, yields should fall to reflect this and so total return would be reduced for buyers.

On the other hand low rental growth need not indicate poor performance. The important analysis is of price against value. The valuation model takes as inputs rental growth forecasts, assessments of depreciation, risk and the required return (see Chapter 4).

These then can be used to forecast returns for each sector/region. They can be regarded as forecasts of return (IRR) or as buy/sell rules (NPV). These forecasts are inputs into portfolio analysis models.

We may suggest that forecasts are necessary and valuable. But there are suggestions from time to time that forecasts are of no value because even government economists make errors. Against this, it can be argued that the process which is created by forecasts is valuable in itself, but there is no denying that bad forecasts can damage performance. What is our experience?

RES, a consulting company now part of the Henderson Investors property team, annually measured the accuracy of its forecasts by measuring the performance of a notional portfolio which is rebalanced annually by sector and region using RES one-, three- and five-year forecasts. The results are shown in Table 3.2.

For the optimised fund, we set a target of half of the total out-performance to be achieved through sector/national structure and a half through sector/region structure. The RES portfolio optimiser model was then run to create an appropriate fund structure. This structure is combined with achieved returns to calculate an outperformance figure. This outperformance figure relative to the

Table 3.2 RES forecasts and notional fund performance (%)

Target	0.5	1.0	2.0
National sectors	0.4	0.9	1.8
Retail regions	0.1	0.2	0.2
Office regions	0.2	0.4	0.9
Industrial regions	−0.2	−0.2	0.2
Regional total	0.1	0.2	0.5
Total	0.5	1.1	2.3
Market risk	0.3	0.6	1.3

Source: Henderson Investors

specified target is a good indicator of the effectiveness of the RES return forecasts.

The heading line posits the required level of outperformance against the index. The first line of the table for national sectors represents the fund outperformance relative to the benchmark produced by the bets at the sector/national level. The next four lines represent the outperformance at the sector/region level as if each sector/region were a separate fund plus the total figure, which is the regional outperformance figures adjusted by the IPD sector weights. The total outperformance, reported in the penultimate line, should be compared with the target.

On average over the three years from 1991 to 1993, the optimised fund would have achieved or exceeded its objective. The majority of this favourable performance is attributable to correctly ordered forecasts at the sector/national level. A further but smaller contribution derives from favourably ordered forecasts at the sector/region level, although incorrectly ordered forecasts at the regional level for industrials detracted slightly from performance in two out of the three years.

Naturally, as the target performance increases, so does fund risk (tracking error: see Chapter 6).

However, transaction costs which are the product of sector switches that are not necessary for stock selection or active management purposes will reduce the outperformance estimates by up to a half. This suggests that managers using forecasts in this simplistic way need to double the bets taken against the benchmark to achieve their structure-based return objective.

3.9 Valuations without forecasts

Property markets are not efficient. As a result, it may be possible to identify cheap or dear markets. Inefficient local markets can at certain times produce forecastable excess returns for investors using rational decision models, even without rent forecasts.

For example, consider office markets across Europe. In very simple terms, given economic and market fundamentals, the following factors, among others, are likely to hold for a set of non-domestic markets:

- Rents look low against other global markets.
- Capitalisation rates look high against other property markets.
- Capitalisation rates look high against other asset classes in the same domicile.
- Capitalisation rates look high against other asset classes in the home market.

For example, in 1991 office rents in Central London had fallen by some 50% from the high levels of 1989, yet the other major European capitals stood at all-time high rents. Given that capitalisation rate differentials had remained broadly the same over the period and given reasonably similar demand and supply fundamentals (vacancy rates, economic growth forecasts and so on), an allocation choice between London or a set of non-UK markets was clear. London was cheap relative to these markets – and, sure enough, it outperformed over the period.

In these circumstances an insightful valuation procedure is every bit as valuable as a good set of forecasts.

Similarly, the concept of rent pressure – a means of identifying markets where rents are higher or lower than spatial, demographic or economic fundamentals suggest – has been successfully applied by a small number of investors across UK towns for several years, with powerful performance implications.

In Chapters 5 and 6 we go into more detail regarding the delivery of performance.

Chapter 4

The Purchase Process

4.1 Introduction

Buying and selling properties involves the following crucial stages. First, the ideal portfolio structure needs to be determined. Once this target structure is in place, the manager needs to identify which market sub-segments are attractively priced and should be targeted. Next, stock needs to be sourced from the market and appraisals of the available properties need to be undertaken. In addition, the impact of proposed purchases on portfolio risk and return needs to be modelled. In the acquisition process, negotiation skills need to be employed, and due diligence needs to be carried out. It is also necessary to think about the demands placed on the investor when selling property.

In this chapter, we make only passing reference to the separate skills and disciplines of marketing and negotiation, and to the sales process. Instead, given the very great importance of stock selection in the delivery of performance, we concentrate on the appraisal and (to a lesser extent) the due diligence process in property acquisitions.

In Chapter 3 we discussed one of the portfolio strategy objectives, namely to create a structure for the portfolio to achieve the return and risk objectives. This would normally be by reference to market segment, such as regional location and sector type (for example, City offices). The identification of target market segments can be a more detailed process.

The identification of attractive market subsectors, cities and districts of cities, or of market themes likely to be associated with excess returns, is the subject of Chapter 5. In brief, however, it may be possible, without taking large sector or locational bets, to associate high returns with market segments or tilts, such as large/small, new/old, in town/suburban, short leases/long leases.

Many property fund managers pride themselves on their access to stock, due either to a large scale of operation leading to a high number of transactions being offered, or on their carefully nurtured relationships with brokers in the market. Buying 'off-market' has become a watchword for doing good deals, and consultants who advise on manager selection are often very concerned with a fund manager's access to market information and buying opportunities. This is dealt with in section 4.2 below.

Much has been written about this subject in academic textbooks (see for example Baum and Crosby, 1995). It is normally the case that an investor will have a target rate of return for an asset and will use a discounted cash flow approach to judge whether a property is likely to achieve that target. We concentrate on some of the more practical aspects of appraisal in sections 4.3–4.7 below.

Individually assessed target returns fail to take account of the impact of the transaction on the portfolio, either in terms of its risk or indeed of the return impact. This needs to be the subject of a separate exercise. This is dealt with in section 4.8 below.

In the purchase process, due diligence describes the legal, physical and planning enquiries and explorations prior to exchange of contracts and completion that are necessitated by the unique nature of the asset type. This is dealt with in section 4.9 below.

4.2 Sourcing stock

The property acquisition process may, in the coming decade, be transformed by the Internet. All vendors of property investments may access a common website, post details of the properties they wish to sell as well as the types of properties they are interested in buying, until something approaching a centralised market may become established. Until that happens, the investment property market will remain decentralised, inefficient and dependent upon the interpersonal skills of buyers and sellers operating in the complex market web of telephone, e-mail and socialising.

Skills are needed by fund managers and buyers as well as by brokers and vendors. After all, every property asset has a degree of locational monopoly. The potential buyer will need to be able to command loyalty from brokers if he or she wishes to access the appropriate quantity and quality of deals. This will often depend upon his perceived trustworthiness in following through on offers.

Brokers can act as very effective agents for vendors if they are able to establish a relationship with their clients, as well as improving the efficiency of the market by matching buyers and sellers and recommending buyers who are most likely to proceed with the deal at the required price.

Typically, fund managers will use a property registration system to record the invitations to treat which are delivered in the form of posted or faxed particulars. Once acknowledged, this will determine the broker's right to charge a commission on completion of the sale.

Brokers may be retained by vendors, which means they will not seek commissions from purchasers. Alternatively, they may act on an unretained basis, seeking a commission from the purchaser and expecting to undertake advisory analysis work to help the client to make an informed decision. The quality of this advice will increase the chances of repeat commissions, just as the quality of the purchaser's follow-through will increase the quality of offers from retained and especially unretained agents, who will lose the opportunity to act for another purchaser if they spend too much time advising their first choice.

Vendors will use their brokers to help decide on the appropriate course of action when offers are made. A contract may be offered to a purchaser at a certain price, but whether this happens will depend not only upon the price offered but also upon the buyer's trust-worthiness and creditworthiness and the quality of other offers. Often, a second buyer will be kept in the wings in case the due diligence process throws up a reason – or excuse – for the purchaser to renegotiate or 'chip' the price.

The subtleties of this process make its complete substitution by a successful Internet-based trading market unlikely for larger and more complex commercial property, certainly for some time. The use of such systems for registration of introductions, information transfer and monitoring of marketing programmes is more likely to be quickly accepted.

4.3 Appraisals

The property appraisal process is reasonably well understood. The modern investor will typically buy in or undertake research aimed at enabling a view to be formed of rental growth and movements in yields, usually derived from a view of the economy and other capital markets.

Computer-based appraisal models will usually be fed with projected rents and yields. The investor's view of the value of the asset will typically be arrived at using discounted cash flow, with internal rate of return the typical buying rule despite a clear preference among academics that net present value produces a superior decision. It is not surprising that a total return or IRR measure is used in appraisals when the manager's objective is framed in terms of a total return, but the IRR rule may produce suboptimal decisions. (Even NPV can be criticised by those familiar with option pricing techniques.)

International investors and property companies may be more interested in the return on equity after tax and tax allowances: see Chapter 8.

The property types and segments described in Chapter 1 have differing qualities which are translated into the price paid for a standard unit. It is sometimes useful to describe property prices in terms of a single unit price per acre, hectare, square metre or square foot; more often, prices are described in terms of initial or equivalent yield.

In theory the standard multiple applied to the unit of rent could more usefully be used as a unit of comparison. For example, a retail property leased for £100,000 a year, which sells for £2 m, shows a multiplier of 20. This property would be regarded as superior to one whose multiplier was 12.5.

However, the reciprocal of the multiplier (100% divided by the multiplier), known as the initial or all-risks yield, is the common measure used. Hence a retail property leased for £100,000 rent a year which sells for £2 m shows a multiplier of 20 and more importantly a yield of 5%; an industrial property leased for £100,000 a year which sells for £1.25 m shows a lower multiplier of 12.5 and conversely a higher yield of 8%.

Why would a purchaser of typical industrial property require a higher initial income per £100 invested (and therefore pay a lower multiplier) than he would from a prime retail property, or, in other words, what makes an industrial property less attractive to a purchaser? One way of attacking this problem is to use a constant growth model, which suggests that (assuming yields do not change) the initial yield is a function of the total required return less the net growth in income which is expected.

The total required return is itself a function of the risk-free rate and a risk premium; the net income growth is a function of the rate of rental growth expected for new buildings in the market and the rate of depreciation suffered by a property as it ages. (This is explained in more detail below.)

The closest available proxy for the *risk-free rate* is the yield to redemption on fixed interest gilts. The cash flow is certain, the investment is liquid; it is cheap to manage.

The *risk premium* covers factors such as:

- uncertainty regarding the expected cash flow, both income and capital;
- illiquidity relative to gilts;
- management costs.

Growth is the rate at which the rental value of a new building at some date in the future is expected to be higher than the current rental value of a new building. It can be separated into two components: growth in line with inflation and 'real' growth, that is growth in excess of general inflation.

Depreciation is the rate at which the rental value of a property falls away from the rental value of an otherwise similar new property as a function of physical deterioration and of functional or aesthetic obsolescence (see Chapter 2).

Table 4.1 shows how typical yields for good quality properties in the major segments may be explained by different values for these variables. In each case the risk-free rate plus the risk premium comprise the required total return from the investment, or hurdle rate; from this rate is deducted the expectation of net rental growth (inflationary growth plus real growth less depreciation) to produce the appropriate initial or all-risks yield. If future changes in yields are ignored, note that the total return expected for the investment is the initial yield plus net rental growth. The basis of this approach is explained in more detail in section 4.4 below.

4.4 Valuation models

It is important to distinguish between three concepts:

- *value*: the underlying investment worth of an asset, or the true equilibrium price of an asset traded in a market where full information is available;
- *price*: the market's estimate of value;
- *valuation*: in property usually an estimation of price but strictly an estimate of value rather than price.

This section establishes a basic framework for the estimation of the value or worth of an asset and how it can be compared to price for buy and sell decisions.

The value of an investment is the present value of its expected income stream discounted at a rate which reflects its risk. However, any estimate of value depends on the views of the investor making the estimates. Price may differ from value:

Table 4.1 Indicative sector/region yields

Sector	RFR* + %	Risk premium = %	Inflation + %	Real growth − %	Depreciation + %	Initial yield %
Standard shops	5.5	2	2	1	0.5	5
Shopping centres	5.5	3	2	1	1.5	7
Retail warehouses	5.5	2.5	2	1	0.5	5.5
Central London offices	5.5	2	2	0	1	6.5
Secondary offices	5.5	4	2	0	2	9.5
Industrials	5.5	4	2	−1	1.5	10.0

Note: * risk free rate

- if the vendor has to make a forced sale for any reason;
- if the investor is better able to use the available information; or
- if the investor has different views.

4.4.1 *The Fisher equation*

The Fisher equation considers the components of total return on an investment. It states that:

$$R = l + i + RP$$

where:

R is the total required return
l is a reward for liquidity preference (deferred consumption)
i is expected inflation
RP is the risk premium.

'l' is given by the required return on index-linked gilts (let us assume 2.5%). '$l + i$' is the required return on conventional gilts (for simplicity, ignoring an inflation risk premium: let us assume 6%). These may be regarded, respectively, as the real and nominal risk-free rates (RF_R and RF_N). (Note that $RF_N = RF_R + i$, assuming there is no inflation risk premium, so i appears to be 6% − 2.5% = 3.5%. If an inflation risk premium of 1% is assumed, the rate of expected inflation implied by a comparison of index-linked and conventional gilt yields is 2.5%.)

Let us assume that RP is 3%.

The Fisher equation can then be rewritten as:

$$R = RF_N + RP$$

R is 6% + 3% = 9% in this case.

4.4.2 *A simple cash flow model*

Consider a simple nominal cash flow:

I is the constant income, received annually in arrears.
R is the discount rate (the required return, consisting of a risk-free rate (RF_N) and a risk premium (RP))

Then investment value (V) is found as follows:

$$V = I/(1 + R) + I/(1 + R)^2 + \ldots + I/(1 + R)^n + \ldots$$

The discounted cash flow is a geometric progression which simplifies to:

$$V = I/R$$
$$\text{or } I/V = R \quad \text{(the correct yield)}$$

It is then possible to compare R with I/P (the *current market* yield) to determine if the asset is mispriced. This is a simple valuation model which ignores the possibility of income growth. In equilibrium, the current market yield would be 9% in our example.

4.4.3 Gordon's growth model (constant income growth)

Expected income growth became embedded in the behaviour of equity and property investors by the late 1950s in the UK. It became necessary to extend the simple cash flow model by introducing a constant rate of growth in nominal income (G_N). Let us assume 3% constant growth in rents.

$$V = I/(1 + R) + I(1 + G_N)/(1 + R)^2 + I(1 + G_N)^2/(1 + R)^3 + \ldots$$
$$+ I(1 + G_N)^{n-1}/(1 + R)^n$$

$$V = I/(R - G_N)$$

$$\text{or } I/V = R - G_N \quad \text{(the correct yield)}$$

It is then possible to compare $(R - G_N)$ (9% – 3% = 6%) with I/P (the current market yield).

4.4.4 A property valuation model (depreciation)

The analysis can now be extended by introducing a constant rate of depreciation (D). This gives (approximately):

$$I/V = R - G_N + D \quad \text{(the correct yield)}$$

Let us assume a constant depreciation rate of 2%. It is then possible to compare ($R - G_N + D$ = 9% – 3% + 2% = 8%) with I/P (the current market yield).

Alternatively it is possible to compare the required return:

$$R = RF_N + RP$$

with the expected return:

$$I/P + G_N - D$$

The comparison of required return with expected return is equivalent to comparing correct yield with current yield. The correct yield is 'value' and the current yield is 'price'.

In more simple terms, let us call the initial yield K.

Then, in equilibrium, and assuming annual growth in rent,

$$K = R - G_N + D$$

and

$$\underset{\text{required return}}{RF_N + RP} = \underset{\text{expected return}}{K + G_N + D}$$

When markets cannot be assumed to be in equilibrium:

if	$K > R - G_N + D,$	buy;
if	$K < R - G_N + D,$	sell;
if	$RF_N + RP > K + G_N - D,$	sell; and
if	$RF_N + RP < K + G_N - D,$	buy.

In our example, let us assume a current market yield of 7%. In this case:

$$7\% < 9\% - 3\% + 2\%, \text{ and}$$
$$6\% + 3\% > 7\% + 3\% - 2\%$$

so the market is a sell.

This is a simple framework, assuming that property behaves as a pure equity investment with annually reviewed rents and (in addition) perpetually flat yields. The real world is somewhat more complicated. Rents are fixed for periods of time. As a useful progression from this simple world, therefore, property should be regarded as a combined bond and equity investment.

This complexity needs to be reflected in the two component parts of an appraisal. These are the cash flow forecast and the discount rate.

4.5 The cash flow

All property investments have bond components to the cash flow. Between rent reviews, the income is fixed. The expected cash flow from a property investment is therefore a combination of bond and equity. Even a heavily over-rented office has an equity component at the lease end, and a retail warehouse has a bond component between reviews. Property is a hybrid, and the appraisal must reflect this.

The cash flow must also reflect the following factors.

1   Property is also subject to the lease which determines the payment of rent. For example, the reversionary nature of some

property investments will create an income uplift at the next review.

2   Property, more than any other mainstream investment, is a tangible asset which depreciates through physical deterioration and obsolescence.

The over-rented component of the cash flow will be subject to greater risk than the portion secured by the estimated rental value or ERV; separation of the cash flow into these two component parts would therefore be wise.

The holding period used in cash flow projections should normally coincide with a lease end or review. However, this may not always be the case. In any event it should be determined with care for several reasons. These are as follows.

* The net present value (NPV) or internal rate of return (IRR) (see Baum and Crosby, 1995) will not be invariant with regard to the holding period.
* The shorter the holding period, the greater the influence of the exit value, which will be a more risky input.
* The manager may have an expected holding period, which may or may not equate with lease ends or reviews.

4.6 The discount rate

The discount rate applied to the cash flow from an investment should be the required return, made up of a risk-free rate and a required risk premium. Simplistically, the risk-free rate is the redemption yield on gilts for the matched life. To be accurate, the yield curve should be taken into account for incomes of different timing.

The required risk premium should be determined by the liquidity of the investment and by the sensitivity of the cash flow to shocks created by inaccurate forecasts or unforeseeable events.

For the equity component, that is the exit value or the uplift at review, the sensitivity of the cash flow to economic shocks will be very important indeed. For those investors interested in the real cash flow, shocks to inflation may be important.

For the bond component, assuming no default risk, the sensitivity of the nominal cash flow to economic shocks is nil. Default risk is, however, highly relevant, and will be the most important factor in the risk premium. Shocks to inflation will affect bonds more than equities, because the cash flow is fixed in nominal terms and therefore has no inflation-proofing quality.

In addition, all property is subject to the extra illiquidity which affects all property much more than normal bonds and equities and which will lead to an increase in the risk premium.

Certain research systems include the provision of a series of risk premiums for subsectors of the property market, defined by use sector and subsector, by region and by town. Where a sale or purchase is being assessed and the present value or net present value over purchase or sale price needs to be estimated, these systems establish a broad guide for estimating the risk premium which might be used in the discount rate. However, where an individual interest in property is being appraised, a further set of considerations needs to be taken into account.

This section summarises one system in current use which measures the issues relevant to the assessment of the individual or specific risk premium. Three main categories of premium drive the specific risk premium in this particular system. These are the sector or subsector premium, the town premium and the property premium.

4.6.1 The sector premium

The system described herein assesses the risk premium based on a checklist of issues and using a variety of quantitative and qualitative measures. The starting point is the estimation of a premium for the whole equity-type property sector based on a presumption about the equity risk premium and the relative position of property. Hence the sector premium is based on the following:

- the equity premium; and
- the differential property premium.

Beyond this, the sector premiums are assessed by taking into account three factors. These are:

- the sensitivity of the cash flow to economic shocks, with particular reference to rental growth and depreciation;
- illiquidity; and
- other factors, including the impact on portfolio risk and the lease pattern.

4.6.2 The town premium

The assessment of the town risk premium is based on an assessment of the riskiness of the economic structure of a town and its catchment area, together with a consideration of competing locations. The range expands from a minimum town premium for diversified and liquid towns with healthy industries to maximum premiums for illiquid towns whose economies are concentrated in weak sectors.

Low liquidity scores are assigned to towns and sectors where it is considered relatively difficult to raise cash from a sale at short notice. Hence Cambridge retail – a popular sector – would typically score more highly than Middlesbrough industrials.

4.6.3 *The property premium*

This section deals with the four components of the property premium, as listed below. The four components are:

- the tenant risk class;
- the lease risk class;
- the building risk class; and
- the location risk class.

Some of these factors will be specific to sectors of the market (in-town retail, for example). The relative weighting of the factors can be assessed by multiple regression analysis, whereby (given a large sample of individual property investments) the current importance of these variables in explaining yield or risk premiums can be assessed and their future importance hypothesised.

The simple process is best illustrated by an example.

4.7 Example

We are considering the purchase of either of two City office buildings. Our estimate of the risk premium for a prime City office is 3.25% over the risk-free rate, currently 6%.

Tenant
- The tenant of property A is a FTSE 350 corporate.
- The tenant of property B is a partnership of solicitors.
- Additional premium: 0.5% for building B.

Tenure
- A is leasehold for 63 years, with low gearing.
- B is leasehold for 116 years with no gearing.
- Additional premia: 1.5% for building A; 0.5% for building B.

Table 4.2 Building-specific risk premia: an example

Factor	Building A	Building B
Risk-free rate	6.00	6.00
Base premium	3.25	3.25
Tenant	0.00	0.50
Tenure	1.50	0.50
Leases	0.00	1.00
Building	0.50	0.00
Location	0.00	0.25
Premium	5.25	5.50
Discount rate	11.25	11.50

Leases
- The sublease for A has 18 years to run, with no breaks and upward-only rent reviews.
- B has ten years to run, with no breaks and upward-only rent reviews.
- Additional premium: say 1% for building B.

Building
- A is an inflexible building: extra premium 0.5%.

Location
- B has a location heavily dependent on neighbouring tenants remaining in place: extra premium 0.25%.

Table 4.2 summarises the cumulative effect of these individual adjustments.

For a full worked example, see the case study described in Chapter 10 of Baum and Crosby (1995).

4.8 Modelling the impact on portfolio risk and return

4.8.1 The portfolio model

In the above example, the expected return on each asset would be modelled using a discounted cash flow procedure. The most attractive property will be the one for which the expected return exceeds the required return by the greatest amount. In most circumstances, this process may be optimal. However, in other circumstances it may not.

Table 4.3 Portfolio modelling (1)

Data	Year 0	Year 1	Year 2	Year 3	Year 4	Year 5
Income	£1,500,000	£1,500,000	£1,500,000	£2,050,000	£2,050,000	£2,050,000
ERV	£2,000,000	£2,000,000	£2,050,000	£2,100,000	£2,200,000	£2,220,000
Term to review	3	2	1	5	4	3
Capitalisation rate	7.50%	7.40%	7.00%	6.50%	7.25%	8.00%
Capital value	£25,366,404	£26,201,550	£28,771,696	£32,099,908	£29,733,893	£26,901,093

First, it ignores the impact of tax and gearing. This is dealt with in Chapter 8. Second, it ignores the impact of the purchase on the shape of the portfolio as a whole. Third, it ignores the different outlays involved. Is an excess return of 1% on £5 m outlay superior to an excess return of 0.5% on an outlay of £10 m?

These latter two problems can be dealt with quite simply in a portfolio model. The objective of a portfolio model is to hold forecast cash flows and values, year by year, on all buildings held within the portfolio in such a form as to enable the manager to model the impact of altered expectations on portfolio performance. The model allows scenarios concerning purchases, major expenditure and sales to be explored. Hence, in the above example the impact on portfolio return – and, with the necessary inputs, risk – of the two alternative purchases may be appraised. This deals quite easily with the difference in outlays, as the optimal decision will be the one which (subject to risk) has the greatest positive impact on portfolio return. The impact on the shape of the portfolio and its risk profile is also easily dealt with in the model.

4.8.2 Example

Table 4.3 shows how, assuming rising rental values and varying market capitalisation rates, a single property moving through its five-year review pattern and valued using an annually in arrear equivalent yield approach will vary in capital value. There are three years until the rent review, and market capitalisation rates fall and then rise over the period. The property enjoys a sharp fall in capitalisation rate as it passes through its rent review, reducing the risk to the investor. The property's capital value is sensitive to four variables:

- the income, or rent passing;
- the estimated rental value;
- the period to the rent review; and
- the capitalisation rate.

In Table 4.4 the impact of the changing value and rental income on the total return delivered by the property (see Chapter 6) is shown, based on the following simple return definitions.

Income return is the net rent received over the measurement period divided by the value at the beginning of the period:

$$IR = Y_{0-1}/CV_0$$

Table 4.4 Portfolio modelling (2)

	Year 0	Year 1	Year 2	Year 3	Year 4	Year 5
Capital value	£25,366,404	£26,201,550	£28,771,696	£32,099,908	£29,733,893	£26,901,093
Income		£1,500,000	£1,500,000	£1,500,000	£2,050,000	£2,050,000
Income return		5.91%	5.72%	5.21%	6.89%	7.62%
Capital return		3.29%	9.81%	11.57%	−7.37%	−9.53%
Total return		9.21%	15.53%	16.78%	−0.48%	−1.91%

Capital return is the change in value over the measurement period divided by the value at the beginning of the period:

$$CR = [CV_1 - CV_0]/CV_0$$

Total return is the sum of income return and capital return:

$$TR = [Y_{0-1} + CV_1 - CV_0]/CV_0$$

Table 4.4 shows the results. As the capital value rises and falls, the capital return is strongly positive, then negative. The income return is less volatile. The total return rises and falls in line with changes in capital value.

Combining this data for one property into an aggregate table describing all properties in the portfolio allows the portfolio return going forward to be modelled. Most importantly, different scenarios can be modelled, not only for out-turns of rental growth and capitalisation rate movements, but also for sales from the portfolio, additions of new buildings and so on.

4.8.3 Extensions to the model

For advanced applications, financing and taxation impacts need to be dealt with, and the portfolio model can be adapted to enable regular portfolio monitoring (for example the ranking of expected returns property by property), linkages to portfolio and facilities management systems, and client reporting.

4.8.4 Dealing with risk

The portfolio model can also be developed further into an arbitrage pricing system, designed to explore the sensitivity of portfolio return to various economic and capital market factors such as changes in rates of interest, changes in expected inflation rates, changes in the value of sterling and other relevant factors.

4.9 Due diligence: the building purchase process

In brief, this crucial aspect of the property purchase decision involves the employment of specialist property skills, in-house or out-house, to ensure that the asset being appraised is all that it appears to be.

The introducing agent may be expected to produce an external valuation report, including comparable evidence and opinions concerning the strength of the local market. Whether this can be regarded as impartial professional advice will depend upon the broker and the buyer's relationship with him. For some buyers, especially where debt is concerned, a truly independent valuation may be commissioned.

Often a purchase will be subject to board approval: a true corporate board in the case of property or special-purpose companies, or an internal committee in the case of most institutions. Surveys, dealing with building structure and in some cases with land contamination, are likely. Finally, legal advice will be used to check ownership and the quality of the lease contract and the purchase contract.

Successful stock selection is, in the view of many professional managers, the key to outperformance. This is certainly true in many cases, but the broader picture is examined further in Chapters 5 and 6.

Chapter 5

The Outperforming Real Estate Manager

5.1 Introduction

Property investors, increasingly, use performance measurement and benchmarking services. They exist, first and foremost, to show whether a portfolio has achieved a rate of return better or worse than the 'market' average, or has met investment objectives specified in a more sophisticated fashion. After benchmarking has answered the question 'by how much did we out-(under-)perform the benchmark?' there is an inevitable demand for 'portfolio analysis' which addresses the question 'why did we out-(under-) perform the benchmark?'

An ideal system of portfolio analysis would identify the contribution of all aspects of portfolio strategy and management to relative returns. It would separate, for example, profits earned on investments from returns on held properties. These are two distinctly separate activities with different return and risk characteristics, and reflect different features of management 'skill'. Among held properties, relative return may be influenced by anything and everything from the broadest allocation of investment between sectors to skill in selecting tenants, negotiating rent reviews and controlling operating expenses.

In practice, the heterogeneity of individual properties and complexity of property management mean that the contributions of different functions and skills to portfolio performance are hard to disentangle. This chapter is concerned with the one tool – 'attribution analysis' – which is found in all performance measurement systems in a precisely quantified form.

Attribution analysis seeks to separate (at least) two components of a portfolio's relative return. The first is relative return which is due to 'structure' – the allocation of investment to 'segments' of the market with different average rates of return. The second is 'stock selection' – the choice of individual assets within each market segment which have returns above or below the averages for that market segment.

Table 5.1 below shows the performance of an unnamed fund in the late 1980s.

Table 5.1 **Components of performance (%)**

	Fund total %	Sector component %	Property component %	IPD total %
1987	13.3	−5.1	−6.0	24.3
1988	23.8	−2.4	−2.9	29.2
1989	8.3	−2.2	−3.6	14.1

In 1989, for example, the fund showed a return of 8.3%, which was nearly 6% below the average return for the universe of properties measured by IPD (Investment Property Databank, the UK's leading property performance measurement supplier). It was in the 94th percentile in that year. Over the 1980s the fund achieved an annualised total return of 11% against the IPD average of 15%. The management was replaced in 1990.

The poor sector mix (sector component) explained roughly half of the underperformance. The fund was overweight in retail, the underperforming sector over the period; it was particularly overweight in Scottish retail, again a poor relative performer. The remaining underperformance is explained by poor stock selection (the property component). The reason for this is that one very large asset performed very poorly. However, it is misleading to suggest that these are separable factors, because the large asset was a Scottish shopping centre.

Attribution analysis is of growing importance in property fund management − not just in terms of analysis, but also in the specification of investment objectives, the selection of managers and the setting of performance-related rewards. Yet the above example shows that property is likely to present a series of challenges.

The academic and professional literature which deals with attribution of relative returns in property fund management is very thin on the ground. The literature on portfolio analysis for equities − the original source of the attribution technique − is not only surprisingly scant, but sets out several apparently different methods of defining and calculating attribution components. Following that literature, suppliers of property performance measurement services are also adopting conflicting conventions.

This chapter aims to clarify the potential confusion about the application of attribution analysis to real estate portfolios. Its primary objectives are:

- to give a clear statement of the purposes of attribution analysis, and its meaning for real-world property managers;
- to show, using real portfolio data from IPD's performance measurement services, the practical implications of applying different attribution methods.

5.2 Attribution analysis – definitions and methods

The standard approach to the analysis of equity portfolios (see, for example, Hamilton and Heinkel, 1995) starts from three primary contributors to portfolio return: policy, structure and stock. (Unfortunately, the terminology for the last two contributors varies between sources. 'Structure' may alternatively be described as 'timing' or 'asset allocation', 'stock' as 'selection' or 'property score'.)

This chapter concentrates on structure and stock selection. By structure is meant the allocation of portfolio weights to 'segments' of the market – typically but not necessarily defined by a mixture of property types and geographical locations. By stock is meant the selection of individual investments within each segment which deliver returns above or below the average for that segment.

5.3 The choice of segmentation

The simple statement conceals an initial choice in any attribution system which is critical to all that follows: what segments of the investible universe should be used to define 'structure'? Burnie, Knowles and Teder (1998) state that:

> To be useful as a tool for evaluating portfolio management, performance attribution analysis should be carried out within a framework that mirrors the investment policy and the decision-making process particular to the fund under examination. A comprehensive attribution methodology will account explicitly for each key component of the portfolio management process.

In that view, the segment structure should reflect the way in which the managers of each individual portfolio choose to regard the 'structure' of their investible universe – how that universe is broken down for the purposes of analysis, forecasting and setting target weights. In practice, it would be extremely difficult for performance measurement services to operate, as it would not be possible to compare allocation and selection skills across portfolios.

Table 5.2 IPD returns, 1998

Percentile/segment	1	5	10	25	50	75	90	99	Mean	SD	Obs.
Standard shops	−15.5	−5.0	−1.2	4.1	8.3	13.5	21.1	46.7	9.5	11.5	4,221
Shopping centres	−5.0	0.1	2.9	6.9	11.1	16.3	20.8	27.6	11.4	7.3	259
Retail warehouses	−10.3	−2.9	1.4	5.5	9.9	15.0	21.5	42.4	10.8	9.9	738
Stores/supermarkets	−7.4	0.2	3.7	7.6	11.5	17.7	25.2	50.7	26.5	27.3	420
Other retail	−27.7	−4.4	−0.2	5.3	9.3	13.8	24.7	105.8	11.7	18.9	271
Standard offices	−17.6	−3.1	1.3	6.9	11.2	18.2	26.9	64.6	13.3	14.3	2,693
Office parks	−11.2	−1.7	2.8	6.8	10.8	15.8	25.4	46.5	12.4	10.4	242
Standard industrials	−4.5	4.0	7.3	10.2	13.3	18.2	22.0	62.1	14.3	8.8	62
Industrial parks	−6.8	0.0	4.2	8.2	12.4	15.8	21.2	39.9	12.6	8.3	294
Distribution warehouses	−8.7	−1.5	1.7	5.5	9.7	13.5	19.9	34.2	10.0	7.7	223
Other property	−39.2	−10.5	-6.3	1.0	10.5	16.3	31.2	212.5	15.6	35.5	394
All property	−14.9	−3.7	0.3	5.7	10.2	16.1	24.2	55.0	12.3	54.7	11,142

Note: 'Obs.' refers to the number of properties in each segment

Source: IPD

For practical purposes, there has to be a standardised segmentation applied to the attribution analysis of all investors, at least as a first step. One standard IPD system is shown in Table 5.2.

Several considerations bear upon the choice of segmentation: statistical, practical and convention.

- Statistically each segment should contain a sufficient number of properties for the average return to be reasonably robust: that is, each segment should ideally only reflect systematic risk.
- Following on from the previous point, the optimum segmentation of the market is that which statistically explains the most variance in individual property returns.
- Practically, segments most usefully cover property categories or areas for which property market information, with supporting information on (say) demographic and economic factors, is readily available to support analysis and forecasting.
- And, by convention, segments will be most acceptable to investors where they follow the generally accepted ways of dividing and analysing the market: it would be difficult to offer a detailed analysis service in the UK, for example, which did not show City of London offices as a 'segment'.

In real-world performance analysis services, the search for an appropriate segmentation will tend to resolve quite rapidly to a mixture of the dominant property types (shops, shopping centres, offices, industrials) and the geographical areas (either towns or regions) linked either to well-recognised property 'markets', or the city/regional boundaries used in the production of official statistics.

5.4 Style

Property fund managers may adopt asset allocation positions which are different from the segment weighting of the benchmark for a variety of reasons. This may be the result of forecasts driving tactical asset allocation, so that views of likely market returns influence a manager to adopt an underweight or overweight position relative to the benchmark in an attempt to produce outperformance. It may be the result of strategic asset allocation or policy, where issues other than pricing – for example, liability matching – influence the asset allocation mix. It may also be the conscious or unconscious result of the style of the fund manager.

The term is used here in an attempt to reflect more commonly used judgements of investment style in fund management. Is the manager top-down (driven by a view of sectors) or bottom-up (driven by his choice of properties)? Is the manager a value manager or a growth manager? Such style judgements are, we argue, highly applicable in property fund management and yet are rarely used.

This definition of style implies a persistent bias in the property portfolio structure which is the result of preference or of habit. It may lead to long-term outperformance, or it may not. In equities fund management, value managers have produced very poor returns in recent years. Yet it is not to be expected that value managers cease to be value managers. In UK property fund management, large prime stock has outperformed secondary stock in recent years, yet it is not to be expected that smaller active managers (many property companies, for example) will change their style.

Style may be associated with investment houses, with individuals or with funds. Arguably, there is far too little explicit differentiation between house styles in property fund management. This may change.

5.5 Themes

As noted above, segment structure will typically be defined by reference to property use type and broad geographical region. Property fund managers invest in forecasting systems which enable managers to take a tactical view on prospective returns in the market 'segments' which are determined by this classification. It can be seen, then, that definitions of fund structure are of necessity rather stable. This is rational: data shows that use types in the UK have shown persistent cycles of under- and outperformance over a long period, a strong example being the continued outperformance of retail in the early 1980s and the early 1990s.

However, sector (type)/region segments are not necessarily optimal in permitting outperformance by asset allocation.

Table 5.3 shows the mean average deviation between the mean return on the IPD index and the returns across different segment classifications for the Irish market over the period 1986–95. The table suggests that the mean difference between the return on the individual sectors and the market as a whole in each individual year ('the window of opportunity') is less than the mean difference between the return on different age groups within the industrial

Table 5.3 Mean average deviations, IPD Irish funds, 1986–95

Segment	Mean average deviation
Sector	2.70
Locations within retail	4.40
Locations within offices	1.80
Sub-sectors within retail	4.60
Age within retail	4.30
Age within offices	1.30
Age within industrials	5.70
Size within retail	2.40
Size within offices	1.20
Size within industrials	2.40

Source: IPD

market. There is more dispersion of returns across age bands within the industrial and retail sectors alone than there is across the three market sectors, and it would seem that concentrating on age bands across the market would have introduced the potential for greater returns than concentrating on sector choice would have done.

While sector allocations may not, in Ireland over the period 1986–95, present the maximum potential for outperformance, there is no reason why this might not be the case over some future period. An excellent manager may be expected to anticipate when this might be. Equally, he would be expected to anticipate at what point size becomes important – or age. This is what we mean by themes.

The asset allocation process ideally takes account of themes as well as of standard segmentation. These may be new themes – sensitivity to changes in electronic shopping, for example – or they may be standard, such as high yield/low yield. Themes differ from styles, because themes imply no necessary persistence in the manager's preference for segments, and themes differ from structure, because themes imply no persistence in the segment classification nor reliance on external performance measurement standards.

5.6 City selection

An attribution system will preferably be stable and holistic. One major attraction of a regional classification in the UK, for example, is its completeness of coverage of UK property. However, this does not mean that fund managers will more effectively control risk and seek outperformance by categorising their holdings in this way.

A regional forecasting system may or may not be effective in identifying regional markets which will outperform a national benchmark. Even if it is, this may not be of much use to the fund manager, because he/she may not recognise the region as a useful way to think about the market. A more technical challenge to the usefulness of the region is the possibility that there may be greater windows of opportunity within a region than between regions.

The North West of England, for example, has been suffering net outmigration and forecasts for population growth have been negative throughout the 1990s. Within the region are two major cities, Manchester and Liverpool, one of which has strengthened its position in the national hierarchy and one of which has suffered extreme decline. A fund manager is likely to have considerably different views of Liverpool and Manchester; a property forecast for the north-west region is of very limited value to him.

For US and UK cities the windows of opportunity (mean average deviations from the mean) have been considerably greater at the city level than the regional level. In addition, it appears that greater forecasting success has been associated with town or city level work than with regional forecasts. City selection is a vital input into fund management strategy.

However, portfolio structure is difficult to categorise by city. This is not a holistic system, because even if every city and town in the UK were covered by the benchmark's databank there would still be outliers that fall outside defined city boundaries. This presents an attribution problem.

5.7 Calculating attribution scores

IPD records for a large number of real portfolios over a long run of years can give a fuller picture of the results for real portfolios produced by different attribution methods. The contribution of structure to variation in returns obviously depends on the scale of differences in return across market segments. It reached a maximum in the boom and slump of the late 1980s and early 1990s, when there were spreads of up to 30 points between the strongest and weakest markets. Structure accounts for 18% of the variance in relative returns annualised over 17 years, but 42% of the variance in returns over the nine years when the influence of the boom and slump is at its greatest.

The relative importance of structure and stock is as much a matter of philosophy as of statistical evidence. When calculating the attribution scores, there is even disagreement over the appropriate number of attribution components and how they should be interpreted.

5.7.1 *Two or three terms?*

Brinson, Hood and Beebower (1986) identify three attribution components: timing (which is analogous to structure in our terminology), stock selection and an 'other' or 'cross-product' term. The cross-product term is effectively a residual component that, mathematically, reflects an additional combined contribution of timing and selection. Their interpretation of what they term timing and selection components broadly coincides with structure and stock selection components as defined in this book, but they do not offer an explanation of how the 'other' term relates to the objectives or management of the portfolio. Subsequent authors, and suppliers of performance measurement services, divide into two camps. Experts either follow a decomposition method which calculates structure and selection scores that account for the whole of relative returns without a cross-product component, or prefer to incorporate the cross-product term in either the structure or selection component.

According to Burnie, Knowles and Teder (1998) the cross-product term

> represents the interaction of two other attribution effects but which is not itself directly attributable to any one source of active management. It is therefore usually reallocated to another attribution effect or, if it remains isolated, is an ambiguous term whose value may exceed the measured effects of active management, thus rendering analysis results inconclusive.

Liang *et al* (1999) state that the use of a two-component method is recommended

> on the basis of simplicity and ease of interpretation. Little is lost in terms of usable information, and much 'noise' is avoided in efforts to explain the results to persons unfamiliar with the nuances of the calculation.

Hamilton and Heinkel (1995) and the Property Council of Australia, however, follow the three-component route, and go beyond Brinson *et al* in suggesting how the cross-product term may be related to management decisions. So, as put by Hamilton and Heinkel:

> Cross Product credits a manager for overweighting an asset class in which he or she outperforms the properties in that asset class in the RCPI [Russell Canadian Property Index].

The argument, then, is that the cross-product may reward style, when an overweighting in a segment is a persistent bias justified by consistent good stock selection in that segment.

5.7.2 The formulae

The dominant method of performance measurement expresses the performance of the portfolio against a benchmark as a relative return, based on the ratio of the two rates rather than the simple difference:

Relative return = ((1 + Portfolio return) / (1 + Benchmark return) − 1)

So a portfolio return of 10% against a benchmark return of 5% gives a relative return of 4.8%:

Relative return = 1.10 / 1.05 − 1 = 4.8%

This formula ensures that components of return and returns annualised over a run of years maintain consistent relative results, which is not possible if simple differences are used to compare returns. Attribution scores are built up from comparisons of weights and returns in each segment of the market. Separate structure and selection scores in each segment are summed across the portfolio to produce the portfolio level structure and selection scores which account for relative return.

The two- and three-component methods of attribution calculate structure scores in exactly the same way. In each segment:

Segment structure score = (Portfolio weight − Benchmark weight) × Benchmark return

The alternative ways of calculating stock selection scores are as follows.

The two-component attribution method calculates the segment selection score (the current IPD method) as:

= Portfolio weight × ((1 + Portfolio segment return)/(1 + Benchmark segment return) − 1)

The three-component attribution method calculates the segment selection score as:

= Benchmark weight × ((1 + Portfolio segment return)/(1 + Benchmark segment return) − 1)

The difference lies in a single term. The three-component method multiplies segment-relative returns by the benchmark weight, while the IPD method multiplies by the portfolio weight. When calculated on the IPD method, the structure score and IPD selection score in each segment add up to the weighted contribution to relative return. Summed across segments, the structure score and IPD selection score add up to the portfolio's relative return.

In the three-term method, the structure and selection scores do not add up in this way, leaving a 'residual' term, the cross product, which is calculated as:

Cross product = Relative return − ((1 + Structure score) × (1 + Selection score) −1) × 100

The central questions for suppliers and users of portfolio analysis services flow out of the central choice between two or three attribution components, or the flexible combination of both approaches.

- Is there any way of deciding from the underlying mathematics which of these choices is right or wrong?
- How different do the results from different methods look when applied to illustrative examples or a large number of real portfolios?
- Are there features of property as an asset which imply a choice of attribution method different from other assets?

5.8 Results from different attribution methods

Case 1 stands as an example of the differences in the message delivered to a fund manager by different choice of attribution methods.

Case 1

A fund achieved the following result in 1994. Simplifying the arithmetic system for demonstration purposes and using the three-component attribution method:

$$\text{Outperformance } (1.0) = \text{Structure } (0.1) + \text{Stock } (-0.4) + \text{Cross product } (1.3)$$

What do these results signify concerning the relative importance of structure and stock?

If the cross product is treated as part of stock selection, as in the most common two-component system used by IPD and others:

$$\text{Outperformance } (1.0) = \text{Structure } (0.1) + \text{Stock } (0.9)$$

If the cross-product is allocated to structure, as proposed by Burnie *et al* for a portfolio constructed by bottom-up selection of individual assets with passive structure:

$$\text{Outperformance } (1.0) = \text{Structure } (1.4) + \text{Stock } (-0.4)$$

The choice of method is clearly non-trivial in this example. Different methods show results which differ in direction as well as scale.

Case 2

The performance of a European property share vehicle which was managed by a UK fund manager was as follows, net of the effect of cash:

$$\text{Outperformance } (-2.9) = \text{Structure } (-0.1) + \text{Stock } (-2.0) + \text{Cross product } (-0.8)$$

The fund was overweight in countries where stock selection was poor and underweight in countries where stock selection was good, especially the UK. It would not be a surprise to the UK manager to learn that the stock selection score was better in the UK, but it may be distressing for him to realise that the stock selection under-performance was exaggerated by nearly a full point because of fund structure. Did he take account of expected superior UK stock selection in his asset allocation?

5.9 Attribution and portfolio management

It is not clear from the mathematical construction of different attribution methods, nor (pending further tests) from the real-world portfolio results they produce, that one attribution method is superior to another. Instead, they may each be valid, and particularly valid for particular styles of management.

5.9.1 Top-down portfolio building

The two-component method embodies the classic top-down model of portfolio construction. Policy dictates a benchmark against which the portfolio is to be measured, specified in terms of a portfolio weighting by segment. An 'allocator', working with market analysis and forecasts, decides which segments are likely to outperform or underperform the overall benchmark return and (perhaps taking into account relative risks) determines a target weighting for the portfolio. Other things being equal, segments expected to outperform will be overweighted, taking 'bets' against the market. The scale of the bet will depend on confidence in forecasts, perhaps on permitted deviations from the benchmark specific in policy, otherwise on the manager's willingness to accept tracking error against the benchmark.

Once the target weights have been set, the management task passes to a 'selector'. The selector chooses the specific assets to be held in each segment, with the target of choosing assets which are expected to outperform the benchmark average for that segment. In equities, the assets will (most likely) be shares in individual companies. In property, they will (most likely) be individual buildings.

5.9.2 Backing selection skills

A portfolio constructed by backing selection skills offers a more interesting, and probably more common, case. Here managers choose to hold high weights in segments where selection skills are believed to be strong (perhaps on the evidence of track record). Here the task of the allocator is redefined to take account of both the overall performance of market segments and the skills of the selector when setting portfolio weights. In this case, the three-component method of attribution offers a useful distinction between the relative inputs to portfolio performance. As before, the structure score measures the allocator's forecasting ability. The stock selection score measures the selector's skills in the purest form. The cross product measures how far pre-judgements of selection skills have proved to be correct.

5.9.3 Specialist portfolios

A specialist portfolio could be taken as an extreme case of backing selection skills. Here the portfolio is narrowly structured on segments where selection skills are believed to be exceptionally strong, possibly in the belief that such a concentration will in itself improve selection skills. Attribution analysis as it has been defined above may no longer apply to these portfolios, because portfolio structure is defined by 'policy' rather than manager discretion. Under these conditions, an attribution analysis using a standard segmentation would show the benefits or otherwise of the overall policy choice. The performance of the manager is most appropriately measured against a benchmark limited to the segments predetermined by policy. Within those segments, special attribution analysis by subsegment could provide information on the skills applied within that specialist area.

5.10 Conclusions

Attribution analysis of property portfolios is a tool, not a theorem. There are no clear grounds for a definitive choice between attribution methods which lie either in the mathematics of their construction or in the character of the results they will produce. Like any tool, attribution analysis may need to be adapted to different tasks and circumstances, and should be employed only with clear understanding of its function.

In the ideal world, an attribution analysis which was 'carried out within a framework that mirrors the investment policy and decision-making process particular to the fund under examination' might be flexible in choice of benchmark, the segmentation of the portfolio and the benchmark for analysis purposes (Burnie, Knowles and Teder, 1998). The choice of attribution method used in that analysis should also be part of the manager's skill.

Chapter 6

Measuring Performance

6.1 Performance measurement

There are many confusions concerning return measurement in property. This is largely due to the unique terminology which has grown in the property world; it is also due to the unique nature of property, especially its rent review pattern and the resulting reversionary or over-rented nature of interests.

There is also some misunderstanding of the difference between return measures which are used to cover different points or periods in time. Return measures may describe the future, they may describe the present, or they may describe the past.

Measures describing the future are always expectations. They will cover certain periods of time and may, if that period begins immediately, be called *ex ante* measures. An example is the expected internal rate of return from a property development project beginning shortly; another example is the required return on that project.

Measures describing the present do not cover a period, but describe relationships existing at a single point in time (now). An example is the initial yield on a property investment; while this may imply something about the income return likely to be produced by an investment in the future, it is simply the current relationship between the rental income and the capital value or price.

Finally, measures of return describing the past, or *ex post* measures, are measures of (historic) performance. An example is the delivered return on a project.

Performance measurement is a science which deals only with the past. It must therefore be distinguished from portfolio analysis, which is relevant to the present, and to portfolio strategy, which is relevant to the future. It deals wholly with delivered returns, and not expected or required returns.

6.2 Definitions

6.2.1 *The future*

The following definitions are not performance measures. They describe the future.

Equated yield/IRR

This is the expected return using estimated changes in rental value and yield. There are similarities in other investment markets: these include the gross redemption yield in the gilt market.

Required return

This is the return that needs to be produced by the investment to compensate the investor for the risks involved in holding the investment. It is also called the target rate or the hurdle rate of return.

6.2.2 *The present*

The following definitions are not performance measures. They describe the present.

Initial yield

This is defined as net rental income divided by the current value or purchase price. There are similarities in other investment markets: these include interest yield, running yield, income yield, flat yield, dividend yield.

Yield on reversion (UK)

This is defined as current net rental value divided by the current value or purchase price. There is no equivalent in other markets.

Equivalent yield (UK)

This is the weighted average of the initial yield and the yield on reversion. It can be defined as the IRR that would be delivered assuming no change in rental value, but this has created difficulties in the case of over-rented properties. As in the case of all IRRs, the solution is found by trial and error. There is no equivalent in other markets.

Reversionary potential (UK)

This is the net rental income divided by the current net rental value or vice versa. There is no equivalent in other markets.

6.2.3 The past

The following definitions are performance measures. They describe the past.

Income return

This is the net rent received over the measurement period divided by the value at the beginning of the period.

$$IR = Y_{0-1}/CV_0$$

Capital return

This is the change in value over the measurement period divided by the value at the beginning of the period.

$$CR = [CV_1 - CV_0]/CV_0$$

Total return

This is the sum of income return and capital return.

$$TR = [Y_{0-1} + CV_1 - CV_0]/CV_0$$

Time-weighted rate of return

This is the single rate of compound interest which will produce the same accumulated value over more than one period as would be produced by the component single-period interest rates. Some commentators refer to this as the geometric mean rate of return.

The TWRR ignores the timing of cash injections and extraction. It is appropriate for quoted unitised and other co-mingled funds. It is an inappropriate measure where the manager has discretion over cash flows or cash investments.

Table 6.1 Life fund (fund A)

	Initial value £m	Value at year end £m	Net income £m	New expenditure £m
1997	123.45	94.51	9.34	17.86
1998		165.50	10.12	1.45
1999		177.09	10.32	

Table 6.2 Pension fund (fund B)

	Initial value £m	Value at year end £m	Net income £m	New expenditure £m
1997	12.35	9.53	0.93	0.00
1998		14.00	1.01	1.45
1999		16.50	1.03	

Internal rate of return

This is the most accurate and complete description of historic return. It is appropriate for managers who have discretion over the cash flow and takes into account the cash invested in each period. It is not, therefore, a mean of annual returns.

Money-weighted rate of return

This is effectively the same measure as the IRR. Its use was legitimised by investment professionals seeking an approximation prior to the development of desktop computing facilities. Given that IRR calculations are now straightforward, there is little justification for continued use of the term.

MWRR/IRR is appropriate for funds where the manager has control over cash flows. It takes account of the amount invested in each period – hence the name.

6.3 Example

The returns on two funds, life fund A and pension fund B, were measured over the period 1997–99 (see Tables 6.1 and 6.2). The

Table 6.3 Life and pension fund performance

Year	Life fund %	Pension fund %
1997 total return	−15.88	−15.30
1997 IRR	−16.68	−16.03
1999 total return	12.25	13.46
1999 IRR	12.74	14.04
1997–99 TWRR	13.85	14.82
1997–99 IRR	14.67	13.87

following performance information is available about these funds.

At the year end, the fund managers decide whether or not to buy new buildings and all expenditure takes place at that time.

Expenditure is not taken into account in the year-end valuation completed immediately before each expenditure. It is assumed instead that expenditure adds to the portfolio value at the beginning of the following year.

The results are as shown in Table 6.3.

6.3.1 IRR, TWRR, total return or MWRR?

The life fund achieved a higher IRR over three years than the pension fund. However, the pension fund achieved a higher TWRR.

In 1997, the IRRs achieved by both funds were less than the total returns achieved. In 1999, they were both higher.

Which of these measures is appropriate?

IRR or TWRR?

The life fund appears to have outperformed on an IRR basis because the IRR (which is money-weighted) reflects the additional investment made by the fund at the start of the strong year of 1998. There was extra cash outlay in 1997, but this led to a much higher value in 1999 and a stronger return over the period.

However, the pension fund achieved a higher TWRR (which is not money-weighted), in other words a higher average annual return.

The responsibility for investing the cash determines the correct measure. Who decided to put more money in at the start of 1998? If the decision were the responsibility of the fund managers in each case, then the IRR is correct and the life fund outperformed. If the decision were the responsibility of a higher authority, then the TWRR is correct and the pension fund outperformed.

In addition, it should be noted that the IRR exceeds the TWRR for both funds because on average more money was invested in the better years and/or the initial poor years of performance badly damaged the investment base for the TWRR calculation. This will not always be the case.

IRR or total return?

In 1997, the IRRs achieved by both funds were less than the total returns achieved. In 1999, they were both higher. The differences in each case are simply the result of the timing of rental income, assumed to be quarterly in advance.

Normally, that is when returns are positive, the quarterly payment of rent is an advantage and produces a higher IRR than total return. The total return effectively assumes a single end-of-year rent payment. In this case the IRR assumes that the (quarterly) intermediate cashflows are reinvested at the IRR. Hence the 1999 returns are higher on an IRR basis than on a total return basis. On the other hand, negative returns in 1997 mean that the reinvestment of quarterly income led to negative interest, a damaged IRR and a relatively higher total return.

Total returns are approximations to IRRs, which are certainly superior measures. However, it is more practical to measure total returns. Comparison of IRRs with total returns can be misleading. Professional performance measurement agencies, such as IPD, adjust for the timing effect in their total return calculations.

IRR or MWRR?

The IRR is a perfect mechanism for the measurement of fund return. The MWRR is an approximation to the IRR which was developed because it allowed manual solution by simple algebra or calculator. It is now wholly redundant.

6.4 Capital expenditure

Performance measurement organisations in the UK and US typically use total return measures for single-period performance measurement for all assets. The simple formula is as follows:

$$TR = [Y_{0-1} + CV_1 - CV_0]/CV_0$$

Property causes particular problems rooted in its unique nature as a physical asset class. Capital expenditures will be necessary from time to time to repair, refurbish, extend and improve property. How should this be dealt with?

There are two alternatives. This can either be dealt with as a reduction in income or as an increase in capital invested.

6.4.1 Reduction in income

Strict comparability with equities would suggest that minor capital improvements (CI) should be financed out of cash flow, just as a company would use cash flow to maintain its capital assets. The appropriate treatment is then quite simple. The income return is reduced by the expenditure while the capital return may be increased if the expenditure adds value to CV_1.

$$TR = [(Y_{0-1} - CI) + (CV_1 - CV_0)]/CV_0$$

6.4.2 Increase in capital invested

However, it can be argued that capital improvements are not always minor, and that major improvements – say, extending a building – are similar to purchasing new assets. The appropriate treatment would then be to say that the amount of capital expended adds to CV_0 (and to CV_1 as long as the expenditure adds value) but does not affect the income return.

$$TR = [(Y_{0-1}) + (CV_1 - \{CV_0 + CI\})] / [CV_0 + CI]$$

6.4.3 Timing of expenditure

These examples effectively assume that the expenditure takes place at the beginning of the year. This may not be true; for example, it may take place in stages during the year. The formula can then be adjusted to take account of timing.

For example, using the capital invested approach, expenditure at the half year stage can be dealt with by suggesting that half of the expenditure is invested for the year.

$$TR = [(Y_{0-1}) + (CV_1 - \{CV_0 + 0.5 \times CI\})] / [CV_0 + 0.5 \times CI]$$

Both IPD in the UK and NCREIF in the US currently use variations of this formula. However, there is now a lobby in favour of the first measure (reduction in income). The effect can be significant: while the total return is unlikely to be much affected, the income return can go down (and the capital return can go up) by as much as 2% over typical periods. This raises an interesting question about the income return delivered by depreciating property assets. Do conventional approaches disguise depreciation and overstate income returns?

The argument over these approaches will continue.

6.5 Risk-adjusted measures of performance

A measure of the ten-year returns to UK property companies over the period 1981 to 1992 carried out at Reading University (Ackrill, Barkham and Baum, 1992) showed both Rosehaugh and Mountleigh to be in the top quartile. Unfortunately, both called in receivers shortly after the end of the measurement period. While we know that past performance is no guide to the future, was past performance really no indicator of this prospect?

Happily, it was. Although the average return on these companies was very high, the high returns were concentrated in the early years of the measurement period, and the volatility of the returns from year to year was very high indeed.

A simple means of adjusting the return measure by the volatility of returns was used in the Reading study. The result was that both Rosehaugh and Mountleigh fell into the bottom quartile on a risk-adjusted basis, alongside Speyhawk, Greycoat and other casualties of the early 1990s crash. The risk-adjusted performance measure turned out to be an excellent predictor of failure.

However, just as returns can be calculated in different ways, risk adjustments can be made in different ways and often with different results.

In the following example two fund performances over five years will be compared with that of the UK property market, represented by the IPD annual index. Fund A outperforms by 1% every year. Fund B has the same average outperformance, but behaves more erratically (see Table 6.4). Its volatility of return is higher.

The most commonly used measure of volatility is the standard deviation. One simple route to risk adjustment, then, would be to divide the average return by the standard deviation of that return. This is the reciprocal of what is commonly called the coefficient of

Table 6.4 Fund A or fund B? (1)

Year	IPD	Fund A	Fund B
1	8	9	14
2	15	16	11
3	25	26	28
4	28	28	26
5	4	5	6
Average	16	17	17
SD	9.32	9.32	8.58

Table 6.5 Fund A or fund B? (2)

	IPD	Fund A	Fund B
Average return	16	17	17
Standard deviation	9.32	9.32	8.58
1/CV	1.72	1.82	1.98

Table 6.6 Fund A or fund B? (3)

	IPD	Fund A	Fund B
Average excess return	0	1	1
Standard deviation	9.32	9.32	8.58
1/CV	0	0.11	0.12

variation (CV) and ranks fund B as superior to A, which in turn is superior to IPD (see Table 6.5).

However, the fund manager may not be concerned about absolute volatility of performance. If he is measured relative to IPD, he may be concerned about relative performance. Dividing average outperformance by standard deviation of return produces the same ranking (see Table 6.6).

However, this is now comparing apples with pears; the relevant risk measure is now the standard deviation of relative performance – or tracking error. Dividing outperformance by the tracking error gives a more useful measure (see Table 6.7).

Table 6.7 Fund A or fund B? (4)

	IPD	Fund A	Fund B
Average excess return	0	1	1
Tracking error	0	0	3.58
1/CV	0	Infinite	0.28

We now have the most appropriate ranking of performance for two managers each trying to beat an index. Fund A has achieved consistent outperformance with no tracking error – infinitely good risk adjusted performance. Fund B is less successful.

This is not, unfortunately, the end of the story. Had fund B achieved very slightly higher returns, which would have been best? How much tracking error compensates for an extra unit of outperformance?

In the (amended) words of Dugald Eadie, formerly of WM, a performance measurement company, risk is not an *ex post* concept: who cares about volatility when the money is safely tucked away in the bank? This debate may be redundant – but, if we believe that the past is any guide to the future as it was with Rosehaugh and Mountleigh, we are unlikely to throw these measures out, and further thought will be necessary.

6.6 What causes returns?

6.6.1 Introduction

If investors have perfect foresight, the return delivered on an asset in an efficient market will always be the return they require to make them invest. The purpose of this final section is to explore why delivered returns are not always the same as required returns, using commercial property as an example.

6.6.2 What is a required return?

Any investment should deliver a return which exceeds the risk-free rate by a premium, which in turn compensates for the loss of the disadvantages of the asset class. These are best summarised as risk, illiquidity and other factors (see Chapter 4).

The easiest starting point for considering opportunity cost is to look at a risk-free asset. In nominal terms, this is represented very well by a UK conventional gilt. In real terms, it is represented in the UK by an index-linked gilt.

Whichever is used, the required return is therefore given by:

$$(1 + RF_N) \times (1 + RP) \qquad (6.1)$$

or, as an approximation:

$$RF_N + RP \qquad (6.2)$$

where RF_N is the redemption yield offered by the appropriate gilt and RP is the extra return – the risk premium – required to compensate for the disadvantages of the asset.

While RF_N can be measured by examining the redemption yield offered by gilts, the required risk premium on any asset is expectations based and is therefore harder to estimate. For equities a reasonable estimate might currently be 2.5% (see County NatWest, 1992).

The link between real and nominal risk-free rates is given by Fisher (1930) (see Chapter 4). The return available on index-linked gilts selling at par is the coupon plus realised inflation. The real return therefore equates closely with the coupon, and current averages are around 4%. This is defined by Fisher as the reward for time preference. Investors, according to Fisher, also require a reward for expected inflation, or investment in real assets would be preferable and paper-based investments such as conventional gilts would sell at lower prices. Hence if 8% were available on 15-year gilts, this might include 4% for inflation and 4% for time preference. In Fisher's terms:

$$R \quad = l + i \qquad (6.3)$$

where:

R	= required return
l	= time preference
i	= expected inflation

However, for an investor interested in real returns (say an immature pension fund) conventional gilts are less attractive than index linked gilts. There is a risk of inflation expectations not being realised, so that higher than expected inflation will lead to lower than expected returns, and second, there is a general discounting of investments where investments are risky. In a market dominated by investors with real liabilities, risky (in real terms) conventional gilts would be discounted, meaning the required return would be higher. If required returns equal the available return in an efficient market, then the 8% available on a conventional gilt must include a risk premium. Following Fisher again, the full explanation of a required return is:

$$R = l + i + RP \tag{6.4}$$

where:

RP = risk premium

For conventional gilts, it is possible that:

$$8\% = 4\% + 3\% + 1\%$$

when inflation is expected to run at 3% and the extra return required to compensate investors for the risk that it does not is 1%.

6.6.3 What is the delivered return?

Returns are delivered in two ways: through income (income return) and through capital (capital return). These combine to create total return:

$$TR = IR + CR \tag{6.5}$$

where:

TR = total return
IR = income return
CR = capital return

Income return over any period is the relationship of income delivered over the period and the capital value of the asset at the start of the period:

$$IR = \frac{Y_{0-1}}{CV_0} \tag{6.6}$$

where

Y_{0-1} = income over the period
CV_0 = capital value at the start of the period

$$CR = \frac{CV_1 - CV_0}{CV_0} \tag{6.7}$$

where:

CV_1 = capital value at the end of the period

Capital values can be explained in terms of the relationship of the initial income on an asset and its multiplier:

$$Y \times \frac{1}{K} \qquad (6.8)$$

where:

Y = current income
K = initial yield on the asset

Hence capital values can change where incomes change or where initial yields change. Following Gordon (Brigham, 1985):

$$K \qquad = R - G_N \qquad (6.9)$$

where:

G_N = expected income growth.

To take an example: assume a stock has a current yield of 5%. The required return is 10%, incorporating a 2% risk premium over conventional gilts. It is priced at £20 with an expected initial dividend of £1. The expected growth in income is given as follows:

$$K \qquad = R - G_N \qquad (6.9)$$

$$5\% \qquad = 10\% - G_N$$

$$G_N \qquad = 5\%$$

If expectations are correct, what total return will be delivered? Remember the required return is 10%.

$$TR \qquad = IR + CR \qquad (6.5)$$

$$IR \qquad = \frac{Y_{0-1}}{CV_0} \qquad (6.6)$$

$$\frac{£1}{£20} \qquad = 5\%$$

$$CR \qquad = \frac{CV_1 - CV_0}{CV_0}$$

What will CV_1 be? In one year, if expectations are correct, the income will have grown to £1.05. If initial yields do not change – and because nothing else is assumed to have changed, then initial yields will not change – then the value is given by:

$$CV_1 = \frac{Y}{K}$$

$$= \frac{\pounds 1.05}{5\%}$$

$$= \pounds 21$$

$$CR = \frac{\pounds 21 - \pounds 20}{\pounds 20}$$

$$= 5\%$$

$$TR = IR + CR$$
$$= 5\% + 5\%$$
$$= 10\%$$

The delivered return is equal to the required return, because expectations turned out to be correct.

6.6.4 Why are delivered returns different from required returns?

It should be clear from the above that there are only two reasons why delivered returns can differ from required returns. First, expectations of income growth can turn out to have been incorrect. Second, initial yields might change.

Incorrect expectations of income growth

Let us assume that the income grows not at 5% but at 10%. What will happen? Capital value in year one will be given by:

$$\frac{\pounds 1.10}{5\%} = \pounds 22$$

$$TR = 5\% + \frac{\pounds 22 - \pounds 20}{\pounds 20}$$

$$= 15\%$$

Changes in initial yields

Let us assume now that the income grows as expected at 5% but that initial yields fall from 5% to 4%. Capital value in year one will be given by:

$$\frac{£1.05}{4\%} = £26.25$$

$$TR = 5\% + \frac{£26.25 - £20}{£20}$$

$$= 36.25\%$$

Why do changes in initial yields happen? Given, following Gordon (Brigham, 1985), that:

$$K = R - G_N \tag{6.9}$$

and following Fisher, that:

$$R = l + i + RP \tag{6.4}$$

which simplifies to:

$$R = RF_N + RP \tag{6.10}$$

then:

$$K = RF_N + RP - G_N \tag{6.11}$$

and there are three reasons why initial yields would change: the risk-free rate might change, the risk premium might change, or expectations of income growth might change.

Assuming constant risk-free rates, which is a realistic assumption over the recent past, two more likely reasons are changes in the premium or revised expectations of growth.

Changes in the premium

If the risk premium changes, the initial yield will change by an equal amount. Hence initial yields will fall to 4% if the premium falls by 1% to 1%.

$$K = RF_N + RP - G_N \tag{6.11}$$

$$4\% = 8\% + 1\% - 5\%$$

Changes in expected income growth

If expected income growth changes, the initial yield will change by an equal and opposite amount. Hence initial yields will fall to 4% if expected income growth rises by 1% to 6%.

$$K = RF_N + RP - G_N \qquad\qquad (6.11)$$
$$4\% = 8\% + 2\% - 6\%$$

6.6.5 Summary

Delivered returns will differ from required returns where the risk free-rate remains constant if:

1. expectations of income growth are incorrect at time t;
2. expectations of income growth change at time $t + 1$; or
3. the risk premium changes at time $t + 1$.

6.6.6 Example

Let us assume the required return on office property is currently driven by a risk premium of 3% and that this has been a constant over the past decade. The required return on offices in 1992 would have been around 12% (conventional gilts were yielding around 9%). Why, then, were returns as low as –10%?

1. *Were expectations of office rental growth incorrect?* The out-turn was a fall in rental values of around –20%. This was almost certainly much worse than expected.
2. *Were expectations revised?* It is a natural tendency for market participants to revise expectations based on immediate past experience. This is sometimes described as adaptive behaviour or adaptive expectations (see Chapter 2). The crash in rents in 1992 may have led to gloomier short-term expectations for 1993, no matter how irrational this might have been. It may be equally likely – and rational – for expectations to improve as levels fall.
3. *Did the risk premium change?* It is highly probable that there was an upward revision to the risk premium on offices in 1992. Canary Wharf went into liquidation, Rosehaugh and many other office-based property companies called in the receiver and the sentiment towards offices weakened significantly as rents crashed by more than expected. While such emotions may not

be rational, it is often the case that the realisation of a worst fear creates a new, even worse fear, rather than a feeling of relief. Such may have been the case for UK offices in 1992.

In quantitative terms, let us assume the following. Average income growth of 3% was expected, the required return was 3% over the 9% gilt rate, and initial yields were 9%.

$$K = RF_N + RP - G_N$$
$$9\% = 9\% + 3\% - 3\%$$

Let us add in the out-turn for rents (–20% growth), an increase in the risk premium of 0.5% and an upward revision to growth expectations to 3.5%:

$$CR = \frac{CV_1 - CV_0}{CV_0} \qquad (6.7)$$

$$CV_1 = \frac{Y_1}{K_1} \qquad (6.9)$$

For a building previously earning £1 in rent and valued at £11.11, the new value would be £0.80/K. K would be given as follows:

$$K = 9\% + 3.5\% - 3.5\%$$
$$= 9\%$$

$$CV_1 = \frac{£0.8}{9\%}$$

$$= £8.88$$

$$CR = \frac{£8.88 - £11.11}{£11.11}$$

$$= -20.07\%$$

$$TR = 9\% - 20.07\%$$
$$= -11.07\%, \text{ close to the out-turn.}$$

PART 3

Emerging Markets

Chapter 7

Changing Styles in Real Estate Investment

7.1 Introduction

This chapter (derived from Baum, 1999) sets out to define and describe the forces driving current and emerging styles of real estate investment. In doing so, it draws on a personal view of the global economic forces which have been unleashed as part of the latest industrial revolution. It suggests that these forces have made international real estate investment much more likely to take place, and that this will lead to the innovation of new investment vehicles for the use of the real estate industry.

These economic or market forces include:

- the growth in pension funds;
- the globalisation of business activity;
- the rapid rise of securitisation;
- changes in technology;
- the corporate restructuring which has affected the property industry in line with other corporate sectors.

Real estate is an investment medium, whether in the form of a diversifying institutional asset class, a venture capital vehicle or an industry sector of the global stock market. It is also a factor of production, a place to work, and a place to shop, rest and play. The new market forces have worked on both forms of real estate to create major changes in world property markets. To what extent – and how – will property take part in this process of change?

7.2 The growth in pension funds

Goldman Sachs suggested in 1997 (Griffin, 1997) that the developed world was facing 'a demographic disaster'. The OECD support ratio – population aged 25–59 divided by population aged more than 65 – decreased from 4.5 in 1960 to 3.5 in 1990 and is projected to decrease to 2.5 in 2020. In many countries, the ratio of employed to pensioned will approach 1:1.

As a result of this, global pension funds will be given enormous sums of money to invest over the next 25 years. Goldman Sachs estimates that global pension fund assets (defined as those located in the 15 largest countries) increased from US$4,730 bn in 1991 to US$7,352 bn in 1995 and will exceed US$12,000 bn in 2000. Of the projected increase between 1995 and 2000, US$2,000 bn will constitute investment in new assets. An assumed 8.5% allocation to real estate produces a requirement for global pension funds to invest US$172 bn over five years, or US$37 bn every year.

7.3 Globalisation

Overseas owners are almost certain to continue their recent expansion into the UK commercial property market, and recent activity in France is a sign of the extension of this globalisation of property ownership. International investors are increasingly attracted to listed property vehicles and co-mingled vehicles such as limited partnerships and other tax-effective special purpose vehicles (see Chapter 8).

It is likely that levels of international investment are constrained largely by the number and size of the vehicles available for efficient international investment. As this activity continues to grow, the historic compartmentalisation of real estate into domestic property markets is unlikely to continue. The growth of multinational companies, increased cross-border trade and communication, the dominance of international stock markets and the increasing importance of cross-border benchmarks will all have an impact on the way real estate is leased, bought and sold.

The UK, US, France, Holland and other markets have for some time been countries capable of attracting a wide range of overseas property investors. Most have been particularly attracted to the central business district office markets. The City of London office stock, for example, was domestically owned until Big Bang in the mid-1980s, but levels of overseas ownership now approach 25% (Baum and Lizieri, 1999).

7.4 Securitisation

In the US, the REIT market has grown from tiny market capitalisations to more than $180 bn in eight years, much of it held by overseas investors. From a very small base in 1995 there are now more than 30 listed property companies in Sweden, many with an active international shareholder base. In Australia, rapid growth in the listed property trust market over a ten-year period created a 1999 market capitalisation of $26 bn, representing around 25% of the institutional real estate market.

The Salomon Smith Barney universe of securitised property more than doubled in size through the 1990s. The total market capitalisation of the 400 companies in this index – worth $US250 bn – represents only one-eighth of expected net new pension fund investment in all assets over the period 1997–2002, so the potential for growth is clearly significant.

In an unpublished survey carried out for Henderson Investors in 1996, institutional investors suggested that the greatest deterrent to real estate investment was illiquidity. While it needs to be stated that the survey pre-dated the growth in web-based listing and dealing services, the best remedy for illiquidity was thought to be a public market quotation.

Other surveys suggest similar desires among global investors, and the suppressed demand for securitised real estate product appears to be large. The growth in global securitised property investment seems to be inhibited mainly by a lack of supply, largely created by taxation and regulatory conservatism in markets outside the USA, Australia and one or two other markets.

The potential for development of the European market is great. Germany, France, Italy and Spain (all relatively immature institutional property markets, but all part of a single currency area which has been recently and rapidly projected onto the global screen) have less securitised real estate product per unit of GDP than any other country. The relatively mature markets of the USA, Australia, the UK and Hong Kong have more. The correlation is powerful, and suggests potential rapid growth in European securitisations.

The high fees available for corporate finance engineers create a strong drive from within the world's leading investment banks to promote securitised property products. Given a level playing field in terms of tax treatment, it is easy to conclude that growth in securitised real estate product would be rapid.

Nonetheless, the attractions of traditional direct real estate relative to securitised real estate should not be forgotten. Data varies from country to country, and arguments continue about both the accuracy of real estate data and the ways in which the balance between direct and securitised real estate have changed and will change in future. However, it is clear that securitised real estate offers less diversification than direct or private real estate (see

Chapter 9). This means that it is clearly too early to abandon direct real estate investment to the securities market.

In addition, a comparison of levels of real estate securitisation in the three global regions of North America, Europe and the Asia–Pacific region with the volatility of those markets suggests that increasing levels of securitisation and hence liquidity may be connected with increasing levels of risk, as traditionally defined.

7.5 Changes in technology

Innovation in information and communications technologies is creating gradual change both in the operation of the real estate market and in the usage of space. Internet-based listings of space and investments have been rapidly assembled, and this may well improve liquidity and efficiency. At the same time the nature of space occupation is changing. The growth of employment of information technology support in the City of London, coupled with the growth of information businesses such as Reuters, Bloomberg and others, has to some extent compensated for the decline in traditional back-office banking. While total City employment fell from 384,205 to 320,043 between 1982 and 1995, computer-related and other business activities grew by nearly 30%.

The supply of real estate is not widely considered to be flexible. In the classical model, booms in demand typically create sharp rises in price due to inelasticity. This supposition is being challenged by the rapid development of cyberspace. While the technology revolution may create an economic boom, it may not boost rents. Work in cyberspace (e-mail), leisure in cyberspace (Internet dating), shopping in cyberspace (the shopping channel, e-commerce) and other related developments must all lead to changes if not absolute declines in levels of demand for real estate.

In addition, increasing rates of obsolescence (Baum, 1993; Dixon, Crosby and Law, 1999) will continue to affect owners and the depreciation they are forced to suffer or combat. This factor has encouraged some property owners, both corporate owner-occupiers and investors, to think about selling property to service-oriented real estate managers.

7.6 Corporate restructuring

Merger and acquisition activity, coupled with other forms of corporate restructuring, is tending towards the creation of larger,

Table 7.1 Risk and return: US and UK property and equities, 1978–98

	UK property	UK equities	US property	US equities
1978	25.7	8.6	16.11	6.52
1979	23.0	11.5	20.46	18.48
1980	17.5	34.8	18.09	32.41
1981	15.0	13.6	16.62	−4.91
1982	7.5	28.5	9.43	21.58
1983	7.6	28.8	13.14	22.42
1984	8.6	31.6	13.84	6.10
1985	8.3	20.2	11.24	31.57
1986	11.1	27.3	8.30	18.22
1987	25.8	8.7	8.00	5.18
1988	29.7	11.5	9.64	16.50
1989	15.4	35.5	7.77	31.44
1990	−8.4	−9.6	2.30	−3.20
1991	−3.2	20.8	−5.61	0.54
1992	−1.7	19.8	−4.25	7.69
1993	20.0	27.5	1.20	9.99
1994	12.0	−5.9	6.37	1.33
1995	3.5	23.0	7.55	37.50
1996	10.0	15.9	10.35	22.96
1997	16.8	23.6	13.93	33.36
1998	11.8	13.7	16.13	28.53
Return	12.19	18.54	9.55	17.82
Risk	9.81	12.00	6.88	12.99

Source: Henderson Investors

often multinational corporations. Horizontal, vertical and international integration brings with it the opportunity for ever more specialist management functions, one of the newer forms of which has been corporate real estate management.

Within a major corporation, real estate is unlikely to attract significant investment capital. Corporations are charged with delivering a return on capital invested, and it is unlikely in developed real estate markets that ungeared (unleveraged) returns on real estate investment and development for occupation will match the return from the core activity.

Table 7.1 shows returns to UK and US private real estate and stocks over the period 1978–98: the outperformance of stocks over real estate has exceeded 6% and 8% each year in the UK and US respectively. Hence, for a corporate occupier, reinvestment of the proceeds from the sale of real estate and reinvestment in the core industrial or service activity is likely to be a sound financial decision.

Quite apart from this, the corporate real estate manager tied to ownership or long leases of occupied holdings suffers extreme inflexibility. In the UK, even leasing can be highly inflexible due to long leases with upward-only rent reviews, and the cost of moving is increased significantly by transaction costs.

If the business is locked into owned or leased real estate, inflexibility in accommodation will mean reduced efficiency, in addition to depreciation being suffered by the owner-occupier rather than transferred to the investor.

Under these pressures, there is likely to be a shift in the real estate management industry from full service provision broadly into services for owners and services for occupiers. Financial management for owners is likely to become increasingly specialised and to require the facility to securitise the asset and promote the sale of securities on a global basis. The rise of the US investment bank Morgan Stanley Dean Witter in global real estate investment services characterises this capability.

Facilities management for occupiers – or the provision of corporate real estate services, to use a wider term and concept – is rapidly becoming separable from investment management. The growth of Regus, an international provider of serviced offices and associated service products, is an example of the potential for a new generation of integrators of property services.

Through this period of transition, the traditional full service real estate consultant remains in place, but suffering enormous pressure which has resulted in an epidemic of global mergers (D'Arcy, Keogh and Roulac, 1999).

7.7 Conclusion

Real estate, the factor of production, is suffering a challenge created by the information revolution. The supply of real estate was supposedly limited, but the discovery of cyberspace challenges that view. Shopping by Internet or TV is increasing its share from tiny amounts to an estimated 7% by 2005. The marginal pressure on office space has been relieved by the opportunity to telecommute and hot-desk. Partly as a result of this, occupiers are in a stronger bargaining position, and leases are shorter.

In addition, properties become obsolete and wear out. Buildings need to be refurbished regularly, and some suffer incurable depreciation through being the wrong shape, or of the wrong appearance, at the wrong time. On the face of it, it looks easy to write off real estate as an investment asset. But generalisations such as this are dangerous.

The property market has a built-in resilience which is drawn partly from its essential quality as a factor of production, and partly from the quality of the people who make their living from it. After all, someone has to own the real estate: the essential dynamic will be the transfer of ownership to those with the greatest efficiencies of operation. High levels of professionalism combined with a strong strain of entrepreneurial drive suggest that the market will respond creatively to this latest set of challenges. The response is beginning to be seen in innovation.

Real estate is being converted from its former position as a separate asset class to a very significant sector in the capital markets, in both equity and debt forms. This is already being seen in the US REIT and commercial mortgage-backed securities (CMBS) markets, in the growth of cross-border co-mingled private equity funds and in the creation of property share funds.

Europe and the UK, however, are behind the US, Australia and other markets in their ability to offer tax-effective and liquid property vehicles to the public. Governments will come under increasing pressure, perhaps assisted by European convergence, to enable more efficient vehicles to be created. At that point, should it arrive, specialised providers will offer high quality space to the market and at the same time might begin to provide investors with the opportunity to participate in liquid, high growth equity stocks, alongside more traditional forms of real estate investment.

Chapter 8

International Real Estate Investment: Structures, Vehicles and Performance

8.1 The context

8.1.1 The single European currency

London offers an excellent case study of globalisation (see Chapter 2); changes in the wider geopolitical structure of Europe are equally indicative. European Monetary Union (EMU) is another process of radical change which has been gathering momentum since the Maastricht Treaty (and the planned development of the Single European Market it prescribed) made 1992 a landmark date in European history. The 1999 introduction of the euro as a common currency for 11 countries is the latest major development in that process.

If the UK and other EU countries currently outside the euro bloc join the euro, currency risk will disappear for euroland investors and will be much simplified for non-Europeans. Regulation and taxation rules will slowly begin to converge. Investment benchmarks will become pan-eurobloc. This will create a significant change in investor behaviour: from a position where any exposure to overseas assets is a risk against a domestic benchmark, growing recognition of wider non-domestic benchmarks will lead to a need to invest overseas to *reduce* risk relative to these benchmarks.

As the global pension industry grows and international trading is positively encouraged, international property is likely to become a major asset class. In addition, owner-occupiers are likely to fuel growth in cross-border property investment.

8.1.2 Foreign direct investment

The world is experiencing a fundamental change in the way it trades. The globalisation of business activity is a continuing process, driven both by the conversion of ownership of successful companies from domestic to multinational concerns, and by the increasing opportunities offered to corporations and institutional investors and banks to own overseas assets through globally traded stock markets. The result has been, according to the Economist Intelligence Unit (1997), a surge in foreign direct investment (FDI). Asia–Pacific has been the most popular region for FDI, and in this region real estate investment (the construction of manufacturing facilities, for example) accounted for more than 40% of all FDI. Both occupier demand and the ownership of corporate real estate facilities have become increasingly driven by the needs of the multinational enterprise.

European cross-border investment has been increasing in popularity throughout the 1990s. In the City of London, for example, foreign ownership has risen from around 4% in the mid-1980s to over 20% at 1999. In France, around £3 bn was invested in property by cross-border investors in 1999 alone.

Diversification is a powerful driver of this activity, with the majority of investors seeking higher returns by playing the global property cycle. If returns going forward in the US property market are perceived to be disappointing, US money will look abroad. The rise of international benchmarks and improvements in data provision, coupled with globalisation in general and the growth of the international investment house in particular (examples being GE Capital and Morgan Stanley Dean Witter), have added to the appeal of international investment. Sheer weight of funds drives German funds such as DESPA, which took in over DM2 bn in 1999 alone, to place more than 50% of its investments abroad.

Currency hedging is, however, expensive and difficult to achieve efficiently (Lizieri, Worzala and Johnson, 1998) and vehicles are rarely protected in this way. This problem typically leaves investors at the mercy of currency movements. The use of debt in the local currency (see above) appears to serve a partial hedging function. However, the experience of US investors in Randsworth Trust in 1989, which suffered a complete loss of investors' equity through rising interest rates and falling rents, has served to warn of the dangers of investing in a geared vehicle in an overheating economy.

Other perceived difficulties, including the dangers of operating from a distance with no local representation, are likely to increase the attraction of investing internationally through liquid securitised vehicles. The study of the experience investors have had with REITs at section 8.4 serves to illustrate the advantages and disadvantages of this approach.

Table 8.1 Market definitions

Core	Developing	Emerging
UK	Portugal	Czech Republic
Germany	Spain	Hungary
France	Italy	Poland
Ireland	Denmark	Slovakia
Sweden	Austria	Baltic States
Netherlands	Norway	Turkey
Switzerland	Finland	Greece
Belgium	Luxembourg	Slovenia

8.2 Continental Europe as a real estate market

Most UK investors are likely to look first at investing in continental Europe. This has been true of Commercial Union (France, Poland and others), Standard Life (France, Spain, Belgium) and Scottish Widows (France), and others are likely to follow.

Table 8.1 shows a way to approach this opportunity. It suggests a split of the main countries of Europe into core, developing and emerging markets. Low risk investors would be more likely to go to core markets; high return investors might seek out emerging markets.

The allocation of countries to core, developing and emerging property investment markets is somewhat arbitrary. Nevertheless, broadly speaking, core markets have a benchmark (for the relevance of this, see Chapters 2, 3, 5 and 6), are politically stable, have a stable currency, offer the professional services necessary for institutional investment and are liquid. Developing markets generally have no benchmark, are smaller, have less liquid markets (but liquidity is either growing or is expected to grow) and are politically stable with a stable currency. Emerging markets have low liquidity, less political or currency stability, fewer professional services and no benchmark.

8.2.1 Core

These are defined broadly in terms of all or most of the following criteria: membership of the EU; membership of EMU; political stability; currency stability; generally having a benchmark (the exceptions are Belgium and Switzerland); size; quality of professional services; and liquidity.

Table 8.2 Core and developing countries: return and risk, 1985–97

Market group	Return (%)	Risk (SD, %)
Core retail	12.01	17.56
Developing retail	16.44	25.88
Core office	11.56	17.65
Developing office	13.43	25.76

Source: CB Hillier Parker, author

8.2.2 Developing

These markets are less liquid (although they are likely to have growing liquidity) and have no benchmarks, but are politically stable, either within the EU or EMU.

Using CB Hillier Parker data describing returns notionally available on new buildings, this core/developing classification has been surprisingly meaningful. In both retail and office markets, the group of core markets has shown both lower returns and lower volatility of returns over the period 1985 to 1997, confirming the different market maturities of these two groups. This is shown in Table 8.2.

8.2.3 Emerging

Several funds have already assembled capital to attack these markets, typically desperately short of capital to fund the property development programmes that are needed to support their economies as they emerge from communist influence. Hence high returns may be obtained by pioneer investors, who can limit their risk by the payment of rents in US dollars (Poland) or deutschmarks (Hungary), and by achieving going-in yields as high as 15%.

8.3 Cross-border flows of capital

In 1972, over 94% of the floor space in a large database of City of London office properties (see Baum and Lizieri, 1999) was owned by UK firms, just less than 3% of space was owned by Middle Eastern interests and around 2% was European owned. The survey found no properties owned by German, Japanese or US firms at that time.

By 1997, 21.9% of the buildings covered in the survey were in overseas ownership. Seven per cent of the properties were in Japanese hands, 5% were German owned, 4% were owned by US firms and just under 3% were, as in 1972, in Middle Eastern ownership.

This growth was, in part, the child of mid-1980s financial deregulation. In 1975 the New York Stock Exchange abolished minimum commission rates: 35 broking firms went out of business but stock market turnover exploded. In 1979, UK exchange controls were abolished, allowing capital to move freely around international markets – a move paralleled in other developed economies. By 1986 the implementation of financial deregulation ('Big Bang') meant that merchant banks, jobbers and brokers could combine to become full capacity investment banks, and overseas players could join the London Stock Exchange. Financial business had become global, and London was one of the global financial capitals.

Over the period 1991–96, market globalisation intensified, so that the overseas ownership of UK equities increased from 12% to nearly 17% over the five years to the end of 1996. The overseas acquisition of UK finance houses, culminating in 1994–97 in the purchases of Warburgs, Morgan Grenfell, Barings, Kleinworts, Smith New Court, BZW and Mercury by Swiss, Dutch, German, French and American banks, is explained largely by the need of the City economy to access wider markets.

At the same time, savings-based liquidity in Japan, the relaxing of Swedish and German cross-border investment restrictions and changes in German tax policy pushed funds out from these savings-oriented countries, and much of the money flowed into UK property. DTZ (1999b) estimated that overseas investment in UK commercial property rose from £0.2 bn in 1987 to £1.9 bn in 1988, £3.1 bn in 1989 and £3.3 bn in 1990, remaining well above £1 bn every year thereafter. According to DTZ overseas owners accounted for around 12.5% of all UK commercial property transactions over the period 1988–95: clearly, the City has taken a larger than average proportion of this investment.

The overseas ownership of City office property has increased in line with levels of foreign equity ownership, and there is evidence that by 2000 this had begun to spread into other sectors and regions of the UK market. It has also been estimated that over 90% of investment transactions in the Paris property market over the period 1996–99 involved non-French buyers. At the same time, international capital flowed into major listed property companies, and many professionals (see for example Eichholtz and Lie, 1999) have been strongly promoting the indirect route as the most effective means of achieving international diversification.

To what extent can it be certain that international investment has been effective or beneficial? What are the advantages and disadvantages of direct ownership of foreign property and buying listed property securities? These questions are examined in the following case study.

8.4 Case study: have US REITs been beneficial for investors?

This study examines the evidence of the returns delivered by REITs to investors over the last decade or longer. It sets out to answer three questions:

- Have US REITs been beneficial for US investors?
- Have US REITs been beneficial for UK or European pension funds?
- Have US REITs been beneficial for UK or European property investors?

In this study, the following definitions are used.

- NAREIT is the return series for REITs maintained by the National Association of Real Estate Investment Trusts.
- S&P500 is the Standard and Poor index of the performance of the largest US stocks.
- R2000 is the Russell Company's index of the performance of smaller US stocks.
- 90-day is the return delivered by 90-day treasury bills in the US.
- NCREIF is the return series for private real estate maintained by the National Council of Real Estate Investment Fiduciaries in the US.
- Mean is the arithmetic mean of annual returns.
- SD is the standard deviation of annual returns, a measure of risk.
- Correlation is the correlation coefficient between two variables, with a maximum value of 1 indicating perfect positive correlation, a minimum value of −1 indicating perfect negative correlation and a value of 0 indicating no correlation.
- IPD monthly is the IPD monthly index of UK property returns.
- IPD annual is the IPD annual index of UK property returns.
- FT gilts is the Financial Times index of returns on UK government bonds.

Table 8.3 Stock, bond, real estate and REIT performance, 1979–98 (quarterly)

	NAREIT %	NCREIF %	S&P 500 %	R2000 %	90-day %
Mean	3.17	2.20	4.43	4.11	1.75
SD	7.49	1.84	7.45	10.77	0.68

Source: NAREIT, NCREIF, Datastream

- FTA is the Financial Times/Actuaries index of UK all share returns.
- UK prop shares is the property sector within the Financial Times/Actuaries index of UK all share returns.

All analyses have been carried out using returns in local currency.

8.4.1 Have REITs been beneficial for US investors?

This section sets out to examine the following question: for the multi-asset US investor, for example a US pension fund, have REITs added to return or reduced portfolio risk? Have they been demonstrably superior in these respects to direct US real estate?

Table 8.3 shows that REITs (3.17%) outperformed direct US property (2.2%) over the period 1979–98 by almost 1% per quarter, in return for significantly higher volatility (7.49% against 1.84%). For an investor who requires liquidity, REITs have a great advantage over the private market, but the volatility would be a serious problem. On the other hand, the outperformance may have been enough to compensate for this.

Table 8.3 also shows that REITs have underperformed both larger stocks (3.17% against 4.40% for the S&P 500) and the smaller stock benchmark which is accepted as more appropriate (4.11% for the Russell 2000). Volatility for REITs has been similar to that of the larger stocks, but the Russell 2000 has shown greater volatility (10.77%) than REITs. Comparing REITs with smaller stocks also seems to reveal a fair game: REITs have produced slightly less return for slightly less risk.

Table 8.4 shows that the S&P 500 and Russell 2000 have themselves been highly correlated (88%), and REITs have been reasonably highly correlated with both. REITS, as expected, have attached themselves more to the smaller Russell 2000 benchmark

Table 8.4 Stock, bond, real estate and REIT correlation, 1979–98 (quarterly)

	NAREIT %	NCREIF %	S&P 500 %	R2000 %	90-day bills %
NAREIT	100				
NCREIF	–4	100			
S&P 500	59	–1	100		
R2000	72	–5	88	100	
90-day T-bills	–2	54	–13	–6	100

Source: NAREIT, NCREIF, Datastream

(72% correlation against 59% with the S&P). Private property represented by the NCREIF has offered much greater diversification (effectively nil correlation) against stocks, but while T-bills have been quite highly correlated with NCREIF, they have shown no correlation with REITs. REITs would have been better diversifiers than private property for a fixed interest investor, but slightly less effective than stocks.

REITs have performed like low-risk, lower-return, smaller US companies. They have offered greater returns than the private property market and better diversification against T-bills, but have provided no real diversification against stocks.

8.4.2 *Have REITs been beneficial for a UK multi-asset investor?*

This section sets out to examine the following question: for the multi-asset European investor, for example a UK pension fund, have REITs added to return or reduced portfolio risk? Have they been demonstrably superior in these respects to direct UK real estate?

Table 8.5 shows that for a UK investor exposed largely to stocks, REITs have offered very poor returns (0.53% per month against 1.31%) over the period 1987–99, and have even underperformed UK government bonds (0.89%). The IPD monthly index has also marginally underperformed government bonds, but has outperformed NAREIT, while producing much less volatility (0.89% against 3.45%). The volatility of NAREIT has been slightly less than that of the UK stock market (4.86%), but much higher than the volatility of government bonds (1.04%).

Table 8.5 UK stock, bond and real estate and REIT performance, 1987–99 (monthly)

	NAREIT %	IPD monthly %	FTA %	FT gilts %
Mean	0.53	0.85	1.31	0.89
SD	3.45	0.89	4.86	1.04

Source: NAREIT, IPD, Datastream

Table 8.6 UK stock, bond and real estate and REIT correlation, 1987–99 (monthly)

	NAREIT %	IPD monthly %	FTA %	FT gilts %
NAREIT	100			
IPD monthly	–10	100		
FTA	45	–8	100	
FT gilts	17	–12	12	100

Source: NAREIT, IPD, Datastream

In addition, as Table 8.6 shows, NAREIT has been positively correlated (45%) with the UK stock market over this period, while the IPD monthly has been negatively correlated with the market (–8%). UK property has also been a better diversifier against government bonds (–12%) than NAREIT (17%).

For a UK multi-asset investor, there is no doubt that over the longest period for which monthly data is available UK property has been a better bet than REITs, the only advantage of the latter being liquidity, itself somewhat offset by the problem of currency risk.

The period 1991–99 has clearly been a much better period for REITs, and this is also a period of analysis which is justified by the re-emergence of REITs in the 1991 savings and loan crisis.

Table 8.7 shows that return and risk data for this period places REITs closer to the UK stock market in both monthly returns (0.94% for REITs against 1.43%) and risk (3.43% for REITs against 3.87%). NAREIT marginally underperformed UK government bonds and outperformed the IPD monthly index by 20 basis points per month for a significant increase in volatility in each case.

Table 8.7 UK stock, bond, real estate and REIT performance, 1991–99 (monthly)

	NAREIT %	IPD monthly %	FTA %	FT gilts %
Mean	0.94	0.74	1.43	0.96
SD	3.43	0.72	3.87	1.23

Source: NAREIT, IPD, Datastream

Table 8.8 UK stock, bond and real estate and REIT correlation, 1991–99 (monthly)

	NAREIT %	IPD monthly %	FTA %	FT gilts %
NAREIT	100			
IPD monthly	−31	100		
FTA	78	−57	100	
FT gilts	44	−88	28	100

Source: NAREIT, IPD, Datastream

Over this shorter period, Table 8.8 shows that NAREIT has been even more positively correlated (78% against 45%) with the UK stock market, while the IPD monthly has been much more negatively correlated with the market (−57% against −8%). UK property has also been a much better diversifier against government bonds (−88%) than NAREIT (44%).

For a UK multi-asset investor, there is little to be said for REITs as a diversifying asset: UK property has been much more effective, albeit with less liquidity, but for no currency risk.

8.4.3 Have REITs been beneficial for a UK property investor?

This section sets out to examine the following question: for the European property investor, for example a UK pension fund, have REITs added to return or reduced portfolio risk? Would direct/private US property or UK property shares have been a better diversifier for the UK property investor?

Table 8.9 REIT and UK real estate performance, 1973–99 (annual)

	NAREIT %	IPD annual %
Mean	10.75	12.8
SD	21.31	11.18
Correlation		–53.1

Source: NAREIT, IPD

Table 8.10 REIT and UK real estate performance, 1991–99 (annual)

	NAREIT %	IPD annual %
Mean	12.46	6.8
SD	18.63	9.73
Correlation		–70.3

Source: NAREIT, IPD

Using annual data, Table 8.9 shows that NAREIT (10.75%) has underperformed the IPD annual index (12.8%) by around 2% per annum over the period 1973–99. The volatility of the NAREIT (21.31%) has been close to double that of the IPD (11.18%). This is not good news for REITs.

However, from Table 8.10 it is clear that the diversification potential for a UK property investor has been strong, the correlation over this period being –53%. Over the more recent period 1991–99, the diversification potential increases (a –70% correlation), while the NAREIT (12.5%) has easily outperformed the IPD (just under 7%) for a similar doubling of volatility (18.6% against 9.7%).

Would direct US property have been a more effective diversifier for the UK property investor?

From Table 8.11, the IPD has outperformed both NAREIT and NCREIF by 50 and 100 basis points each quarter respectively over the period 1987–99, with somewhat greater volatility (2.73%) than the NCREIF (1.8%) and, of course, much less than the NAREIT (just over 7%). NAREIT has outperformed NCREIF over the period by 50 basis points per quarter for a significant increase in risk.

Table 8.11 REIT and US and UK real estate performance, 1987–98 (annual)

	NAREIT %	NCREIF %	IPD annual %
Mean	1.96	1.46	2.53
SD	7.05	1.80	2.73

Source: NAREIT, NCREIF, IPD

Table 8.12 REIT and US and UK real estate correlation, 1987–98 (annual)

	NAREIT %	NCREIF %	IPD annual %
NAREIT	100		
NCREIF	−14	100	
IPD annual	−13	39	100

Source: NAREIT, NCREIF, IPD

Table 8.13 REIT and US and UK real estate performance, 1991–98 (annual)

	NAREIT %	NCREIF %	IPD annual %
Mean	3.51	1.35	2.13
SD	7.02	2.09	2.19

Source: NAREIT, NCREIF, IPD

However, from Table 8.12, the risk of REITs for a UK property investor becomes much less in a portfolio context, with a negative 13% correlation for REITs/IPD comparing with a positive 39% correlation for US/UK private property. This in combination with the higher return would have made REITs a significantly better bet for a UK property investor wishing to diversify into the US property market.

Does the more recent period of 1991–98 produce a different story?

Table 8.13 shows that over the more recent period of 1991–98 the picture improves considerably for REITs, which outperformed UK property by nearly 1.4% per quarter and the NCREIF by more.

Table 8.14 REIT and US and UK real estate correlation, 1991–98 (annual)

	NAREIT %	NCREIF %	IPD annual %
NAREIT	100		
NCREIF	−14	100	
IPD annual	−33	35	100

Source: NAREIT, NCREIF, IPD

Table 8.15 REIT, UK property shares and UK real estate performance, 1987–98 (annual)

	NAREIT %	IPD annual %	UK prop shares %
Mean	11.58	10.84	11.96
SD	16.39	9.67	26.83

Source: NAREIT, IPD, Datastream

Table 8.14 shows that the diversification offered by REITs becomes even greater over this period, while the correlation between NCREIF and IPD remains reasonably strongly positive at 35%.

Would UK property shares have been a more effective diversifier than REITs?

Table 8.15 demonstrates that the returns offered by REITs and UK property shares over the period 1987–98 are very similar, at 11.58% and 11.96% respectively. The volatility of NAREIT was, however, considerably lower at 16.4% than that on the FT property share sector (26.8%).

In addition, as Table 8.16 shows, the diversification offered by NAREIT considerably exceeded that offered by UK property shares. The correlation between IPD and NAREIT, at −52%, is of more value to the UK property investor than the negative 23% offered by property shares. This confirms the intuitive notion that international diversification through REITs should be more effective than diversification into domestic securitised products.

There is little doubt that, over the 1990s, REITs have offered excellent potential for the UK property investor to access the US real estate market, to increase portfolio returns and to significantly

Table 8.16 REIT, UK property shares and UK real estate correlation, 1987–98 (annual)

	NAREIT %	IPD annual %	UK prop shares %
NAREIT	100		
IPD annual	–52	100	
UK prop shares	34	–23	100

Source: NAREIT, IPD, Datastream

reduce portfolio risk. This would not have been possible using the private US market. Using UK property shares would have been slightly less effective than using REITs.

The liquidity offered by REITs has been an additional bonus, while the currency risk introduced by REITs may suggest greater attractions for similarly liquid UK property shares than the data reveals.

8.4.4 Conclusions

- REITs have performed like low-risk, lower-return, smaller US companies, offering greater returns than the private market and better diversification against T-bills, but no real diversification against stocks.
- For a UK multi-asset investor, there is little to be said for REITs as a diversifying asset: UK property has been much more effective, for no currency risk.
- There is no doubt that, over the 1990s, REITs have offered excellent potential for the UK property investor to access the US real estate market, to increase portfolio returns and to significantly reduce portfolio risk. This would not have been possible using the private US market. The price of the liquidity offered by REITs has been negative.
- Using UK/US data as a case study, the case for REITs for an international investor is much more powerful when addressed to the property investor seeking international diversification than for the multi-asset investor.

The case for international diversification is not yet made: but we can guarantee that the fee-earning motivation of global real estate managers will present many opportunities for global investors to successfully, or unsuccessfully, attack this new area.

Chapter 9

Emerging Markets: Real Estate and the Capital Markets

9.1 The search for the perfect vehicle

The fundamental problem confronting property investors and property investment managers in the UK and many other European countries is this: to achieve a diversified, liquid property portfolio which offers reasonable returns and diversification against stocks and bonds. In the coming decades all sorts of property vehicles will be offered as solutions to this challenge. At the same time industry groups will be specifying the ideal product and lobbying government to produce changes in tax and listing rules which will enable the ideal vehicle to be created.

No matter what the ideal vehicle might be, many other inferior but successfully marketed fee-producing products will be launched by entrepreneurs and fund management houses. We will see corporate structures, trusts, limited partnerships; open ended and closed ended vehicles; public listed vehicles and private unquoted vehicles; sector-specific derivatives and synthetics; and more that have already been envisaged and many more that have not.

The success of these vehicles will be as much to do with timing, marketing, human behaviour and politics as it will be to do with logic and efficiency. But this does not prevent us from seeking the ideal.

9.2 The paradox

What features would the ideal property vehicle have? It has to be recognised that institutional investors dominate the savings and investment industry. It is also unarguable that equity investment dominates the portfolios of institutional investors and has outperformed property in simple return terms by a large margin for a long time.

The case for property therefore has to be made primarily against equities, and it has to be very strong. Given this, what might make real estate attractive to these investors?

Three qualities of real estate make it attractive to the institutional investor (see Chapter 1). These are as follows:

- It offers the multi-asset manager the opportunity to outperform benchmarks in the short term.
- It reduces portfolio risk in the long term (it has low volatility and diversifies equities and bonds).
- It may help the investor to match long-term liabilities.

What makes real estate unattractive?

- It is illiquid.

This may not be the only problem with property, but it is clear that investors crave liquidity. Many recent reports have shown that investors would pay a premium for a real estate vehicle that was as liquid as the equity and gilt markets are reckoned to be. So the ideal property vehicle offers outperformance, diversification, inflation hedging and liquidity: but there is a price for liquidity.

In a rational world, the return delivered on an asset will be the same as the return investors require (see Chapter 6). This is partly why, in the long run, equities have outperformed gilts – and why they are expected to continue to outperform gilts (see Chapter 2). They are riskier, have a higher required return and (unless we know better) are likely to deliver a higher return.

Property is illiquid. This means that its required – and expected – return is higher than it would otherwise be and, with shorter leases on the way, possibly higher than the required return on equities. Removing illiquidity is therefore likely to remove (say) one percentage point from the long-term expected return on property. This is not a good thing.

So introducing liquidity may damage returns. The yield on properties is as high as it is partly because there is an illiquidity reward. The natural required total return on property is higher because of liquidity and returns would fall if illiquidity did not exist.

Liability matching for pension funds is very closely related to inflation hedging. We regard property as a partial inflation hedge, better over the longer term. Liquidity may introduce volatility and slightly reduce the inflation hedging qualities of property closer to the inflation hedge quality of an equity.

The largest impact of improved liquidity, however, would be upon risk (see section 9.4 below) and diversification. Surveys have consistently shown that diversification is a powerful driver for pension funds and insurance companies to get involved with real estate as an investment. Diversification surely works only as long as the asset is truly different. Is real estate really different from other assets? Why should it behave any differently from pure equity when, after all, it should be driven primarily by the real economy? It was suggested in Chapter 2 that three factors make real estate a different asset.

- *The supply side.* The supply side can be both regulated and inelastic, and will sometimes produce different return characteristics for property than those for equities – which is otherwise the natural property analogy – in the same economic environment. A good harvest will damage the price of wheat in a strong economy, just as oversupply held back office returns in the recovering mid-1990s economic environment.
- *Security of income.* Rent is a superior claim on a company's assets than are dividends. In addition, leases determine the delivery of income and produce short-term bond characteristics with longer-term equity performance.
- *Property's physical or commodity characteristics.* Commodities are by nature different from paper assets. In addition, commodities will normally depreciate over time, they can have a value in use which sets a floor to the minimum value, and they are generally illiquid. Finally, they may have to be valued by experts rather than priced by the market: examples include property of all types (that is, real and personal).

So property is a diversifier away from equities because it has bond and commodity characteristics. Taking away the long lease and the physical, heterogeneous, commodity nature of real estate would take away a large part of its diversification potential. A quoted, liquid property vehicle will inevitably have performance characteristics that are shared with the equity market.

Arguably, the commodity nature of property is more valuable than the bond linkage. It is interesting to see how an economic shock has the same effect on the gilt market as it does on the equity market. In markets fuelled by the anticipation of government policy responses, bad unemployment numbers can lead to rises in both gilt and equity markets because higher unemployment means that interest rates are less likely to rise and more likely to fall. Wholly rationally, when interest rates rise unexpectedly, the discount rate on expected cash flow rises and the price of all assets – except property, of course – falls.

Quoted property vehicles, on the other hand, will go up and down with the market – while property as a commodity, traded outside the securities markets, need not.

We can go some way towards supporting this view by examining the case of property shares, which appear to be good examples of liquid property assets.

9.3 Do property shares offer the ideal property vehicle?

The ideal vehicle offers the multi-asset manager the potential for short-term outperformance. This means that when property is thought to be cheap, the vehicle is about to outperform. The tactical asset allocation process, running week by week, will require this to be so, or otherwise it will be risky or illogical to go overweight, and a neutral weight or an underweight position will be maintained.

The ideal vehicle also offers long-term diversification. The strategic asset allocation process is driven by the asset liability model, using long-run property data: a vehicle behaving like an equity or a bond will invalidate any allocation to property with the result that no investment in property will need to be made other than as part of an equity or bond portfolio.

So do property shares offer the ideal property vehicle? In short, no. This is because they are less liquid than is generally supposed and they are less like property than they need to be. They do not perform like property in the very short term, so they are of no use for tactical asset allocation, and in the very long term they are as much like equities as they are like property, so they are not of very much use for strategic asset allocation purposes either.

9.3.1 Tactical asset allocation

The tactical asset allocation process is designed to generate performance from short-term expectations of returns at the asset level. Within some organisations, the tactical asset allocation decision is conducted on a weekly basis.

Plotting the total return on a monthly basis of direct property (IPD), property companies (FTSE property companies) and equities (FTSE All Share) shows that property companies and the equity market are very volatile compared with the direct property market (see Chapter 2). This is a bad thing: low reported volatility is what investors want, even if the numbers are massaged by valuers. This has been seen as a 'phoney argument' but, while the numbers themselves may be phoney, they go into the performance numbers nonetheless. And this issue is not only about volatility; it is about correlation as well.

Examining historical monthly returns, volatilities and correlations between property, property companies and equities, it can be seen that property companies are a hybrid between property and equities in terms of short-term performance. They have delivered a return since 1987 only slightly greater than that on property, while being far more volatile than both direct property and equities. And, on a monthly and quarterly basis, the historical return on property companies has been much more similar to that on the equity market than to that on the direct property market.

9.3.2 Strategic asset allocation

The strategic asset allocation process is designed to produce a set of assets that are most appropriate taking into account the liabilities of a pension scheme. The allocation to property is determined using asset liability models and inputs that reflect the nature of the assets in terms of return, risk and correlation. It is therefore crucial to examine the characteristics of indirect property vehicles compared to direct property to assess whether the use of indirect property vehicles within the property portfolio damages the integrity of the strategic asset allocation.

Comparing the longer-term total return on an annual basis of direct property, property companies and equities shows that property companies are a hybrid between property and equities. They have delivered a return since 1971 close to that on property while being far more volatile than direct property, indeed being more akin to an equity. This is broadly true independently of the time horizon.

It can also be seen that the pattern of delivery of the historical return on property companies has been much more similar to the return on the equity market than the return on the direct property market. On an annual basis, the correlation between property companies and the property market is only 20%, while that between the property company sector and the equity market has been around 60%.

Over longer periods there is no clear evidence that property companies become pure property. Over rolling three-year periods, the relationship between property companies and direct property is higher and higher still over rolling five years, although it is still lower than the equity market.

Further, very long-term performance numbers show some frightening results. While the property data used in our 75-year analysis is very thin indeed, it shows that property has performed at wholly different times from equities and gilts, and that equities and gilts have been disturbingly closely correlated. For example, in terms of real returns the best rolling 25-year period in the last 75 years has been the same (1921–46) for equities and gilts but different (1944–69) for property. The worst rolling 25-year period in the last 75 years has been the same (1950–75) for equities and gilts but different (1969–94) for property. Should not pension funds and insurance companies value property more highly for this finding?

So, over all time frames, the equity market has a more important impact on the property company market than the property market does. While not all liquid, quoted property vehicles will perform like property companies (REITs, for example, are restricted in terms of development activity, gearing and payout ratios), it is argued that there is a great danger that this will typically be the case for the quoted property vehicle.

9.4 The two ideal assets

Why are property shares linked in performance terms to the equity market? Because they are part of that market and dealt in that way. How can their performance be uncoupled? By separating their trading from the stock market.

Hence we can achieve either true liquidity or true diversification, but not both. There is no one ideal asset, but there may be two. Because of this, investors are likely to accept two parallel developments in the creation of property investment vehicles. The first is the diversification route. The second is the liquidity route.

9.4.1 The diversification route

The pension fund and the insurance company invest in property to achieve diversification and liability matching. Because diversification will be lost by high volume trading through quotation, these should be unquoted vehicles.

Some liquidity can be achieved by matched bargains or by dealing directly with the manager. This is likely to promote (although it does not necessitate) an open-ended structure. In addition, the ability to deal with overseas investors in addition to domestic pension funds will add to liquidity. Some funds are

> **Box 9.1 The diversifying asset**
>
> | | |
> |---|---|
> | Short-term outperformance | No |
> | Diversification | Yes |
> | Liability match | Yes |
> | Liquidity | No |

established offshore largely to improve liquidity by attracting tax-exempt international investors. In future, it is expected that harmonisation will allow EU pension funds to invest cross-border without penalty, and liquidity will improve greatly as a result.

In addition, there is often a healthy secondary market for units. Property unit trusts or unit-linked pension or insurance products are perfectly adequate vehicles for providing pension funds or insurance funds with a means of diversifying into property. So, of course, are segregated direct portfolios, and limited partnerships may also fit the bill.

Remembering the price of liquidity, it is clear that these vehicles should be expected to outperform any quoted alternative. The investment case is irresistible: more return, less volatility and less correlation mean that there is a danger that these vehicles are more valuable than is recognised.

Box 9.1 summarises their advantages and disadvantages.

9.4.2 The liquidity route

What creates liquidity? A quotation is useful, perhaps even necessary. It acts as a shop window for the clearing-house, advertising the product and encouraging buyers and sellers to transact.

But a quotation is not sufficient to attract the attention of a market maker. Many quoted assets – including many small property companies – will not be taken onto the market maker's books. He will require matched bargains and/or require a large spread from buy to sell price. He is more likely to take stock onto his books if there is a large spread, if there is high market capitalisation of the vehicle, or if he can offset the risk in a derivative.

Market makers are essential to ensure that a market can operate at volume. Hence market makers are important in the delivery of liquidity. They require:

- a large spread between buying and selling prices;
- high market capitalisation;
- derivatives to offset risk.

Speculators or arbitrageurs also need to be attracted to add to market capacity. They also help to provide volume, but they require volatility to encourage them to transact. This will mean that average holding periods become shorter. They also require perfectly standard vehicles that they can understand and arbitrage between. We can now add the following requirements:

- daily quotation of prices;
- standard vehicles.

If liquidity can be achieved in the property market in this way, the demand is likely to become very great. In summary, volume is crucial, and it will be created by large market capitalisation of the combined sector of standard vehicles plus short average holding periods. Short holding periods and volatility go together, hand in glove, and require the participation of market makers, investors and speculators. They in turn will be attracted by large spreads, a large volume of similar vehicles and quotation, plus the opportunity to offset risk through derivatives.

Changes in the savings market will also contribute to the development of liquid vehicles. First, money purchase and portable pensions will lead to more investment money being managed by fund managers with retail outlets (unit trusts, investment trusts). Subject to tax, these can be property vehicles.

Property vehicles such as unit trusts and limited partnerships already exist, but there is little or no trading volume because they exist in an imperfect form and are not quoted. Trading volume will develop if and when the tax-exempt traded property vehicle is permitted. Pension funds which are happy with volatility and wish to make an imperfect tactical property move will buy these vehicles, and so will retail investors wishing to spread risk naively and 'play the property market'. This expansion of demand will create volume.

Volume will come with quotation and volatility – and by market makers being fully involved and making profits. The last thing they will want is for the manager to ensure trading at, or close to, appraised value. This limits volatility, volume and spread. Valuation also means that this is not a true security – and trade will be limited by the lack of comfort felt by the market maker.

Box 9.2 The liquid asset

Short-term outperformance	Yes
Diversification	No
Liability match	No
Liquidity	Yes

They will also feel uncomfortable with the open-ended supply of new stock. How can they know how much of the stock they own? How do they control the risk have they taken onto the books? The liquidity-creating vehicles should be closed ended.

The most popular vehicles will be sector-specific. Going long or short in offices is a tactical matter in which liquidity is the vital issue and where the differences between sectors are more important than the diversification damage caused by quotation.

We can call this is a UKREIT. It will be lowly geared and fully distributing, and more diversifying, as a result, than a property company. Nonetheless, it will be less diversifiying than a property unit trust. Box 9.2 summarises its advantages and disadvantages.

9.4.3 Will there be derivatives?

The UKREIT structure can support a traded derivatives market. These work best when the underlying asset is in a standard form and is perfectly hedged by the derivative, and where the underlying asset is quoted and liquid. Trading is essential in the underlying asset to create volatility, which will in turn create trading in the derivative. Market makers need to become involved in the underlying asset, as they themselves will have a natural demand for the derivative. The derivatives can be sector-specific, especially if the quoted vehicles are.

Derivatives are discussed in more detail in section 9.5 below.

9.5 Property derivatives

A second fruitful line of innovation is the creation of specific derivatives for more efficient property investment. Examples are:

- debt securitisation, including commercial mortgage-backed securities;
- income strips, both fixed annuity and geared uplifts;
- swaps.

9.5.1 Debt securitisation

The value of debt-like property investment was recently evidenced in the UK by the appeal of the fixed incomes produced by over-rented office property in the City of London in 1993–94 by German investors. It has been brought into more recent focus by the activities of Rotch, a property company which has exploited the yield gap between high-yield long-lease property and corporate bonds, and by the securitisation of Broadgate by British Land.

The property-backed debt market in the USA, including the enormously successful public commercial mortgage-backed securities (CMBS) market, is huge. It is possible that American players and others will encourage the securitisation of property-backed debt in some volume in Europe, and as a result that the European property market will enter a new phase.

This change would provide opportunities for corporates and developers to raise finance by selling property-backed debt instruments, either quoted securities or private mortgage-type paper. It would produce interesting implications for the valuation, performance and tradability of residual property interests. This may include swapping.

Can income stripping, income swapping and/or securitisation be employed to increase liquidity in the UK property market by saving transaction costs and delays? If there is potential for an increase in property-backed debt in the UK and Europe, what would this mean for institutional property investment managers? If incomes are securitised or stripped, what derivative products can be sourced from the remaining uplifts and reversions?

The potential users of these instruments are as follows:

- corporate property owners seeking to retain control but to employ capital more effectively;
- institutional property investors and property companies wishing to reduce exposure to markets or assets, to raise development finance or to diversify into new markets where entry costs are high;
- institutional UK and international bond investors who wish to invest in higher yield bonds;

- institutional property fund managers wishing to create high performance funds – or to add to shareholder value – by retaining undervalued uplifts and reversions.

The new instruments must be standardised, popular, well-understood and capable of further development (for example, futures contracts). There must be market volume and a two-way market at all times. They must be traded in large lots. They must be tax-efficient, both in respect of income and capital, and stamp duty. They must not breach trading regulations (for example, insurance company solvency, derivative-trading or gearing rules).

The CMBS market is well covered in many US texts. In this section we concentrate on strips and swaps. Much of this material is derived from Baum, Beardsley and Ward (1999).

9.5.2 Strips and swaps

Swaps are private agreements between two companies to exchange cash flows in the future according to a prearranged formula. The first swap contracts in international capital markets were negotiated in 1981. Now, hundreds of billions of pounds of contracts are negotiated yearly on underlying assets ranging from commodities to equity indices, and from fixed/floating deals to inverse floaters on foreign exchange transactions.

Cash flows from property in the form of rentals lend themselves readily to swap analysis using derivative pricing techniques that are now being applied to real estate in the US, UK and Australia. However, the UK lease structure offers a particular opportunity to explore this means of analysis because of the complex option-like characteristics of the typical institutional lease.

Property cash flows can be readily 'partitioned' using derivative pricing techniques with risk-neutral valuation techniques and Monte Carlo simulation (see Baum and Crosby, 1995). The resultant cash flow 'slices' can be swapped or sold both to enable portfolio diversification between funds and to provide funding for developers and corporate owners of property.

For swap transactions, payments are netted out at the end of the swap period with the property never being sold, thus eliminating the high transaction costs associated with property transfers. In effect, a surrogate property sale can be synthetically structured with reversion belonging to the seller of the swap. For property developers or corporations seeking funding, parties can enter into future or forward contracts to sell the cash flows.

In Baum, Beardsley and Ward (1999) we examine pricing and market infrastructure issues surrounding the establishment of markets in both rental swaps and strips or sales. The paper shows how these concepts might be applied to standard UK leases, and we review the mechanisms and credit risk exposure for

- a 'plain vanilla' fixed or floating interest rate swap; and
- an equity swap.

We show then how such structures might be applied to swapping property rentals using an example of a 25-year lease with (a) upward-only rent reviews and (b) open market rent reviews. Finally, we offer some indicative pricing parameters based on the above model for:

- swapping a five-year upward-only lease on one property for a five-year freely floating lease on another property with the same drift and the same volatility; and
- swapping a five-year upward-only lease on one property for a five-year upward-only lease on another property with different drifts and volatilities.

The examples are based on swaps only. Outright sale of expected rentals may be priced in the same fashion. The markets for strips, swaps and sales of property rentals would solve problems for very many potential participants. Many other advances from this idea are possible, and some are discussed below.

9.6 The applications of strips and swaps

9.6.1 *Alpha and specific risk*

As we saw in Chapters 3 and 5, there are two commonly recognised components of risk and return. These are sector structure and stock selection. Sector structure bets can produce outperformance of an index through tactical asset allocation in return for an increase in tracking error relative to a benchmark, while successful stock selection activity produces 'alpha', the reward for successfully taking on specific risk.

In Chapter 5, Table 5.1, we demonstrated an unsuccessful fund that was overweight in Scottish retail largely as a result of holding one very large shopping centre. The managers were removed. The obvious action taken by the succeeding manager was to sell the shopping centre to reduce tracking error despite a very strong forecast for the sector and the asset. He did so, and missed out on rapid and considerable capital growth from an asset he knew intimately.

One major attraction of a swap instrument would be the opportunity for the new manager to retain the alpha of the shopping centre (its outperformance relative to Scottish retails) while reducing tracking error by retaining the shopping centre but swapping out of Scottish retail index performance. This is one of several potential uses of an active property swaps market (see section 9.6.2 below).

9.6.2 *Property sector/single property swaps*

Assume property company B, a City office specialist, wishes to access shopping centre performance and exit City offices. It might swap returns on its investment in Broadgate, an office complex, for returns on Lakeside, a shopping centre. This would be a property deal with low fees; no actual property exchange would take place. The specific risk of Broadgate would be transferred for the specific risk of Lakeside. This may, however, create a potential conflict of interest for each owner.

Alternatively, to engineer no loss of long-term control, alpha or specific risk, a sector index swap might alternatively be agreed. Company B would swap the City office index for shopping centres to achieve portfolio rebalance or tactical asset allocation, while retaining the short-term alpha/specific risk of Broadgate, the asset it owns and manages. On the other side of the bargain, the shopping centre owner would achieve a similar result.

9.6.3 *Multi-asset level swaps*

Assume fund A wishes to assemble a synthetic property portfolio, with no management responsibility (and no tracking error or specific risk). It might swap all-property total returns for other asset classes: FTSE or LIBOR (the London inter-bank borrowing rate). On the other side of the bargain would be property investors wishing to reduce their exposure. This would provide an alternative to the limited availability synthetic property exposure offered by property index certificates (see Chapter 2).

9.6.4 *International index swaps*

International property investment is difficult primarily because of the specific risk which the foreign investor is forced to take on. International index swaps would allow this to be avoided. If and as the UK enters the euro, the benchmark for UK institutional investors might begin to shift to include non-UK European property. Assume fund C wishes to gain continental European exposure, and to do so swaps the UK index for overseas index(es). It does not take the specific risk of overseas assets, and has no need for specialist local knowledge. It reduces its UK exposure and tracking error without selling buildings, and retains alpha/specific risk in the market it knows best.

9.6.5 *Property derivatives: spin-offs*

An active market in property strips and swaps might not provide the perfect property vehicle, but it will enormously improve the efficiency of the market and almost certainly attract capital into the sector. Dealing in put and call options and traded futures would become possible, as would hedging and going short. Option and derivative pricing techniques would become an essential part of investors' appraisal systems, and property ownership would come to be regarded as providing a series of real and financial options. Swaps in particular would bring access to all segments of the market for all investors and allow quick, cheap and easy-to-achieve tactical asset allocation. Finally, it would encourage managers to specialise in property types to retain alpha without being penalised for the tracking error that inevitably accompanies specialisation in the current climate.

9.7 Conclusions

Looking into the future, the implications of an active property securities and swaps market are substantial. Assuming the creation of property bond issues associated with all major prime sectors and locations it may be possible to use swaps to remove/reduce the liquidity risk from property transactions. By investing in bond, uplift, reversionary and possibly development income streams it may be possible to create portfolio structures for a given risk profile (growth or income). In addition, strategy decisions may be conducted by contracting to swap bond, direct or indirect property income flows without selling the underlying asset. If this becomes reality the complexities associated with the creation of direct international property funds (see Chapter 8) could be avoided.

From time to time there will be anomalies that allow income stripping, swapping or securitisation to enhance performance. To capture this, a standard special-purpose vehicle, a standard market mechanism and a means of assessing the valuation of residual interests are all needed. The undervaluation of remaining uplifts creates an opportunity to enhance performance or to add to shareholder value.

Finally, the increase in liquidity may enhance the reputation of property as an asset class. Weightings may be increased. In this sense the availability of property derivatives may increase the aggregate demand for commercial property.

9.8 Afterword

Property is a factor of production, a place to work and the main input into the production of food. It provides shelter and leisure facilities. It is the essential source of work, rest and play.

For a corporation, property is of key importance as a factor of production. For a bank, it provides ultimate security for the majority of all loans. For an investment institution, it represents a significant source of fees. For the nation, it is the basis of a large proportion of the nation's savings, investments and future pensions. While its performance in the past 25 years has not matched that of equities, it has sufficient advantages in terms of liability matching to continue to be a popular investment class in future.

Forces of change will continue to challenge our perceptions of the place and importance of property. Globalisation is damaging the ability of domestic markets to remain insular. Securitisation is a response to global investors placing more emphasis on the liquidity and divisibility of investments. In tandem with this, more unquoted pooled vehicles will be provided to enable global investors to diversify more effectively.

Technological revolution continues at a pace, with e-commerce creating changes in the way we shop, work and distribute goods. Corporate restructuring in the property sector is inevitable, with more emphasis on service provision (characterised by such new concepts and industries as facilities management), leading to shorter and more flexible UK leases.

A growing and more affluent population is leading to congestion and a re-emphasis on town centres for sustainability and lifestyle. Careful planning and sensitive land management and development are ever more important. Property investment managers will be required to play their part in the efficient management of this global asset.

References and Further Reading

References

Ackrill, A., Barkham, R. and Baum, A. (1992) *The Performance of UK Property Companies*. Department of Land Management, University of Reading.

Antwi, A. and Henneberry, J. (1995) 'Developers, non-linearity and asymmetry in the development cycle', *Journal of Property Research*, 12, 217–39.

Barras, R. (1994) 'Property and the economic cycle: building cycles revisited', *Journal of Property Research*, 11, 183–97.

Baum, A. (1993) 'Quality, depreciation and property performance', *Journal of Real Estate Research*, 8: 4, Fall, 541–66.

Baum, A. (1999) 'Changing styles in international real estate investment', *Australian Land Economics Review*, 5: 2, 3–12.

Baum, A. (ed.) (2000) *Freeman's Guide to the Property Industry*. London: Freeman Publishing.

Baum, A. and Crosby, N. (1995) *Property Investment Appraisal*, 2nd edn. London: International Thompson Publishing.

Baum, A. and Lizieri, C. (1999) 'Who owns the City of London?', *Real Estate Finance*, Spring, 87–100.

Baum, A. and Lizieri, C. (2000) *Space Race: The Contribution of Property Markets to the Competitiveness of London and Frankfurt*. Department of Land Management, University of Reading.

Baum, A. and Sams, G. (1997) *Statutory Valuations*, 3rd edn. London: International Thompson Publishing.

Baum, A., Beardsley, C.J. and Ward, C.W.R. (1999) *Using Swaps to Manage Portfolio Risk and to Fund Property Development*. Paper presented at the RICS Cutting Edge conference, Cambridge, September.

Bjorklund, K. and Soderburg, B. (1997) *Property Cycles, Speculative Bubbles and the Gross Income Multiplier*, Working Paper No. 24. Royal Institute of Technology.

Brigham, E. (1985) *Financial Management, Theory and Practice*, 4th edn. New York: Dryden.

Brinson, G., Hood, L. and Beebower, G. (1986) 'Determinants of portfolio performance', *Financial Analysts Journal*, 42: 4, 39–44.

Brown, G. and Matysiak, G. (2000) *Real Estate Investment: a Capital Market Approach*. London: Financial Times/Prentice-Hall.

Burnie, S. Knowles, J. and Teder, T. (1998) 'Arithmetic and geometric attribution', *Journal of Performance Measurement*, Fall, 59–68.

College of Estate Management (2000) *Destination UK: International Property Investment and the Role of Taxation*. Reading: CEM.

County NatWest (1992) *Solving the Risk Premium Puzzle*. Equity Briefing Paper 26, 29 July.

D'Arcy, E., Keogh, G. and Roulac, S. (1999) *The Internationalisation of US and UK Real Estate Service Providers: Competing for a Global Badge of Quality*. Paper presented to the European Real Estate Society, Sixth European Conference, Athens, Greece.

Dixon, T., Crosby, N. and Law, V. (1999) 'Acritical review of methodologies for measuring rental depreciation applied to UK commercial real estate', *Journal of Property Research*, 16, 153–80.

DTZ Debenham Tie Leung (1999a) *Money into Property*, 24th edn. London: DTZ Debenham Tie Leung.

DTZ Debenham Tie Leung (1999b) *Special Report – Overseas Investment in UK Commercial Property*. London: DTZ Debenham Tie Leung.

Eichholtz, P. and Lie, R. (1999) *Property Capital Flows: Moving the Frontiers*. The Hague: ING Bank/ING Real Estate.

Fisher, I. (1930, reprinted 1977), *The Theory of Interest*. Philadelphia: Porcupine Press.

Grenadier, S. (1995) Valuing lease contracts: a real-options approach', *Journal of Financial Economics*, 38, 297–331.

Griffin, M. (1997) *The Global Pension Time Bomb and Its Capital Market Impact*. New York: Goldman Sachs.

Hamilton, S. and Heinkel, R. (1995) 'Sources of value-added in Canadian real estate investment management', *Real Estate Finance*, Summer, 57–70.

Investment Property Databank (1999) *The UK Property Cycle: AHistory from 1921 to 1997*. London: RICS.

Investment Property Forum (1995) *The Pensions Act 1995 and Property Investment*. London: City University.

Liang, Y., Hess, R., Bradford, D. and McIntosh, W. (1999) 'Return attribution for commercial real estate investment management', *Journal of Real Estate Portfolio Management*, 5, 23–30.

Lizieri, C., Worzala, E. and Johnson, R. (1998) *To Hedge or Not to Hedge?* London: RICS.

MacGregor, B. (1994) *Property and the Economy*. RICS Commercial Property Conference, Cardiff.

Morrell, G. (1993) 'Value weighting and the variability of real estate returns: implications for portfolio construction and performance evaluation', *Journal of Property Research*, 10, 167–83.

Scott, P. (1998) *The Property Masters*. London: E&FN Spon.

Wheaton, W. (1999) 'Real estate "cycles": some fundamentals', *Real Estate Economics*, 27: 2, 209–30.

Further reading

Ball, M., Lizieri, C. and MacGregor, B. (1998) *The Economics of Commercial Property Markets*. London: Routledge.

Barkham, R. and Geltner, D. (1995) 'Price discovery in American and British property markets', *Real Estate Economics*, 23, 21–44.

Barkham, R. and Ward, C. (1996) 'The inflation-hedging characteristics of UK property', *Journal of Property Finance*, 7, 62–76.

Baum, A. (1995) 'Can foreign real estate investment be successful?' *Real Estate Finance*, 12: 1 81–9.

Baum, A. and Schofield, A. (1991) 'Property as a global asset', in Venmore-Rowland, P., Brandon, P. and Mole, T. (eds), *Investment, Procurement and Performance in Construction*. London: E&FN Spon.

Baum, A. and Wurtzebach, C. (1992) 'International property investment', in Hudson-Wilson, S. and Wurtzebach, C., *Managing Real Estate Portfolios*. New York: Irwin.

Baum, A.E., Beardsley, C.J. and Ward, C.W.R. (1999) *Derivatives Pricing Approaches to Valuation Models: Sensitivity Analysis of Underlying Factors*. Paper presented to the European Real Estate Society, Sixth European Conference, Athens, Greece.

Cox, C., Ross, S. and Rubinstein, M. (1979) 'Option pricing: a simplified approach', *Journal of Financial Economics*, 7, 229–63.

Economist Intelligence Unit (1997) *Global Direct Investment and the Importance of Real Estate*. London: RICS.

French, N.S. and Ward, C.W.R. (1995) 'Valuation and arbitrage', *Journal of Property Research*, 12, 1–11.

French, N.S. and Ward, C.W.R. (1996) 'Applications of the arbitrage method of valuation', *Journal of Property Research*, 13, 47–56.

Hendershott, P. (1995) *The Use of Equilibrium Models in Real Estate Research*. London: RICS Cutting Edge (conference proceedings), 351–8.

Hoesli, M. and MacGregor, B.D. (2000) *Property Investment: The Principles and Practice of Portfolio Management*. London: Pearson Education.

Investment Property Databank and University of Aberdeen (1994) *Understanding the Property Cycle: Economic Cycles and Property Cycles*. London: RICS.

Lee, S.L. and Ward, C.W.R. (1999) *Estimating the Volatility of Individual Property Returns*, Working Paper. Department of Land Management and Development, University of Reading.

McGough, T. and Tsolacos, S. (1997) 'The stylised facts of the UK commercial building cycles', *Environment and Planning A*, 29, 485–500.

MacGregor, B. and Schwann, G. (1999) *Common Features in UK Commercial Property Returns*. IRES conference paper.

Renaud, B. (1998) *Property Cycles and Banking Crises*. IPD conference paper.

Schofield, J.A. (1996) 'Inflation hedging and UK commercial property', *Journal of Property Finance*, 7, 99–117.

Schofield, J.A. (1997) 'Commercial property: a model return', *Professional Investor*, September, 20–3.

Scott, P. and Judge, G. (1999) *Cycles and Steps in British Commercial Property Values*, mimeo. Department of Economics, University of Portsmouth.

Sharpe, W. (1988) 'Determining a fund's effective asset mix', *Investment Management Review*, November/December, 59–69.

Thomas, V. (1998) *How to Avoid History Repeating Itself – the Bank of England's Role in the Commercial Property Market*. IPD conference paper.

Tsolacos, S., Keogh, G. and McGough, T. (1998) 'Modelling use, investment and development in the British office market', *Environment and Planning A*, 30, 1409–27.

University of Reading and DTZ Debenham Thorpe (1995) *The Chartered Surveyor as Management Consultant: An Emerging Market*. London: RICS.

Ward, C. and French, N. (1997) 'The valuation of upwards only rent reviews: an option pricing model', *Journal of Property Valuation and Investment*, 15, 171–82.

Ward, C., Hendershott, P. and French, N. (1998) 'Pricing upwards only rent review clauses: an international perspective', *Journal of Property Valuation and Investment*, 16, 447–54.

Williams, J. (1991) 'Real estate development as an option', *Journal of Real Estate Finance and Economics*, 4: 2, 191–208.

Worzala, E., Newell, G. and Lizieri, C. (1996) *The Convergence of International Real Estate Markets*. AREUEAconference paper.

Other sources

Other relevant material may be available at:

www.andrewbaum.com
www.freemanpublishing.co.uk
www.ipdindex.co.uk
www.propertyderivatives.com
www.reading.ac.uk
www.rics.org.uk/research
www.uli.org